THE BIGGEST LIE IN THE HISTORY OF CHRISTIANITY

THE BIGGEST LIE IN THE HISTORY OF CHRISTIANITY

MATTHEW KELLY

BLUE SPARROW BOOKS

North Palm Beach, Florida

THE BIGGEST LIE IN THE HISTORY OF CHRISTIANITY

Design by Ashley Wirfel

ISBN: 978-1-63582-040-9 (hardcover)
ISBN: 978-1-63582-050-8 (softcover)
ISBN: 978-1-63582-061-4 (e-book)

10   9   8   7   6   5   4

Printed in the United States of America

CONTENTS

LIFE IS A PUZZLE

Once upon a time there was a very successful business owner. His company had faithfully served millions of customers for many years. But lately business had not been so good, and his competitors were just waiting for him to fail. For months the man pondered the crisis, but the problems were so complex, and solutions seemed nowhere to be found.

Everyone was wondering what would happen to this great company, so finally the businessman announced that he was hosting a dinner for all of his employees; he would unveil a plan that would save the company and return it to its former glory. He wanted to convey to them how important each person was to the future success of the organization.

The morning of the dinner, he was sitting in his study at home working on his speech, when his wife came in and asked if he would mind watching their son for a few hours while she ran some errands. He was about to say, "I really need to focus on finishing my speech," but something caught his tongue and he found himself agreeing, if reluctantly.

His wife had only been gone about ten minutes when there was a knock on the study door, and there appeared his seven-year-old son. "Dad, I'm bored!" he exclaimed. The father spent the next couple of hours trying to amuse his son while also trying to finish his speech. Finally he realized that if he could not find some way to entertain his child, he was never going to get his speech finished in time.

Picking up a magazine, he thumbed through the pages until he came to a large, brightly colored map of the world. He ripped the picture into dozens of pieces and led his son into the living room. Then, tossing the pieces all over the floor, he announced, "Son, if you can put the map of the world back together, I will give you twenty dollars."

The boy immediately began gathering the pieces. He was keen to earn the extra money, as he needed just twenty more dollars to buy a toy he had been saving for since his last birthday. The father returned to his study, thinking he had just bought himself a couple of hours to finish working on his speech, because he knew his seven-year-old son had no idea what a map of the world looked like.

But five minutes later, just as he was settling into his speech, there was another knock on the study door. There stood the young boy holding the completed map of the world.

The father said in amazement, "How did you finish it so quickly?"

The boy smiled and said, "You know, Dad, I had no idea what the map of the world looked like, but as I was picking up the pieces, I noticed that on the back there was a picture of a man." The father smiled, and the boy continued. "So, I put a sheet of paper down, and I put the picture of the man together, because I knew what the man looked like. I placed another sheet of paper on top, then holding them tightly I turned them both over." He smiled again and exclaimed, "I figured, if I got the man right, the world would be right."

The man handed his son twenty dollars. "And you've given me my speech for tonight. If you get the man right, you get the world right."

***

Transforming people one at a time is at the heart of God's plan for the world. It is also essential to developing dynamic marriages, loving families, vibrant Christian communities, thriving businesses and economies, and extraordinary schools and nations. If you get the man right (or the woman, of course), you get the world right.

Every time you become a-better-version-of-yourself, the consequences of your transformation echo throughout your family, friends, business, school, neighborhood, church, marriage, nation, and beyond to people and places in the future. It is God who does the transforming, but only to the extent that we cooperate. God's grace is constant, never lacking. So our cooperation with God's desire to transform us is essential; it is the variable. Are you willing to let God transform you?

If you get the man or woman right, you get the world right. Such a simple message—yet we seem constantly obsessed with things we have no influence over, rather than focusing on where we can have most impact, which is with our own thoughts, words, and actions. It is our own thoughts, words, and actions that are at the epicenter of our circle of influence. The further we get away from them, worrying about what other people are thinking and saying or doing, the weaker our influence and impact becomes. Focus on affecting what you can affect and you will have the most effect. It all starts with you.

YOUR HAPPINESS PROJECT

Have you ever noticed that everyone wants to be happy? Everyone! Is that just a coincidence? Probably not. At least, I don't think so. I think there is a reason we all have this incredibly strong yearning to be happy. What's the reason? We human beings were created for happiness and more.

In some ways life is a happiness project. This project is full of paradoxes. For example, it may seem like it is about you, but it's actually more about what you can do for other people. It turns out that bringing happiness to other people increases your chances of being happy, while seeking happiness for yourself decreases those chances.

We all do stupid things from time to time, and usually we know they are going to bring us a measure of misery before we do them. They may bring some type of momentary pleasure or adrenaline rush, but these things pass quickly, leaving our yearning for true happiness stronger than ever. Then we try something else, hoping *that* will make us happy.

So, let me ask you: How's your happiness project going? Give yourself a progress report. What's working? What's not working? What wisdom do you have about the quest for happiness that you could pass on to others? And most important, do you feel you have finally unearthed the secret to happiness?

The thing is, our deep yearning isn't for momentary pleasures; it is for lasting happiness in a changing world. The world is always changing; we cannot control every situation. Situational happiness is easy. It is easy to be happy lying on an exotic tropical beach all day for a week. But so much of this happiness is dependent on the situation. What we are really hungry for is a happiness that is independent of the situation.

Paul the apostle had it. He continually wrote about joy in his letters from prison. In fact, it was the most common theme in his writings from the filth and squalor of his first-century prison cell. Could you be happy in that situation? I don't think I could be, if I'm being honest. I'd probably get miserable and depressed pretty quickly. So I am right by your side in this journey with you, and I have a lot of work to do myself. I am also in the midst of my own happiness project, and just like yours, it has its ups and downs. Among authors there is a saying that goes something like, "We write the books we need to read." So maybe I am writing this book for you, or maybe it is the message I most need to hear at this time.

Through my own quest for happiness, there are a few things I have learned:

- Happiness and pleasure are not the same thing.
- Getting what I want doesn't make me happy.
- Focusing on myself almost never leads to happiness.
- I am never happy when I pretend to be someone I am not.
- Too much of the happiness I experience is dependent on unsustainable circumstances or situations.
- The more I help others in their quest for lasting happiness, the happier I seem to be.
- Lying never makes me happy.
- Happiness is always found by embracing the present moment.
- It is impossible to be grateful and unhappy at the same time.
- Anything that helps me become a-better-version-of-myself makes me happy, even if it is difficult or painful.
- Happiness is contagious.

You have no doubt discovered your own truths about happiness that could be added to this list. But there is one question that I want to ask you as we begin this journey together: Do you believe it is possible to be happier than you have been at any other time in your life? Think about that. Don't just read on. Pause for a moment and reflect. Do you believe it is possible to be happier than you have ever been?

I believe it is. And I am going to show you how in this short book. So stay open to this one possibility.

Real happiness is a sign that the human spirit is thriving. This is the thriving I yearn for and the thriving I suspect you are hungry for. We want to live life more fully; we're impatient to live life to the fullest. So wherever your happiness project is right now, even if it is a complete train wreck, all I am asking you to do right now is open yourself to the possibility that God wants you to experience a happiness greater than you have ever experienced before in your life. Stay open. Together we are about to discover something wonderful!

THE FALSE PROMISES
AND LIES OF THIS WORLD

Modern culture is constantly feeding us lies and false promises.

Let me share something with you about me: I don't like being lied to. This is not unique or special. Do you like being lied to? I didn't think so. I also don't like being lied about. One of the hardest things to come to grips with once you put yourself out in the world as a public figure is that people will shamelessly, recklessly spread lies about you, seemingly without giving it a second thought. I suspect you don't like being lied about either.

Now, it may bother you less than it bothers me, and it may bother someone else even less than it does you, but nobody likes it. I don't know a single person who enjoys being lied to. I also don't know a single person who likes being lied about. In fact, a person who wants to be lied to would be considered mentally ill.

One of our culture's most prominent lies is that there are no universal truths. Modern secularism is built on the lie that nothing is true for everyone. And yet, with a relatively simple example—nobody likes being lied to—we seem to have debunked that lie.

The world's promises of happiness are false promises, and a false promise is a lie. Our secular culture's philosophy about life and happiness can be most succinctly summarized in this way: The meaning of life is to get what you want; and the more you get of what you want, the happier you will be.

We know it's a false promise. We know it's a lie. Still, we fall for it over and over again. How often do we convince ourselves consciously or subconsciously that if we get the car, the dress, the bag, the watch, the job, the guy, the girl, the house, the trip ... we will be happy? This leads to two outcomes. The first is bad but not as diabolical as the second. The first outcome is we get the car, for example, and for a few days or weeks we are delighted and completely enamored with it. Getting the car has brought some measure of happiness, but that happiness is circumstantial; it is dependent on the car. If the car were taken away, the happiness would evaporate. In fact, we would probably be even unhappier than we were before we ever got the car. That's the first outcome—we get the car, it brings a measure of happiness, and that happiness soon fades.

As I mentioned, the second outcome is even worse. In scenario number two we don't get the car, the job, or the girl, and we spend the rest of our life in a self-imposed victimhood believing that if only we had gotten the car, the job, or the girl, we would have been happy forever. The person who never gets the car never works out that the car was never going to make him really happy. So he lives perpetually in the false promise.

Getting what you want doesn't make you happy. This is true for many reasons—for one, you simply never can get enough of what you don't really need.

Why do we fall for these false promises of happiness so easily and so often? There are a thousand reasons, but primarily it comes down to the fact that we can be very lazy and we are attracted to the promise of easy happiness. It seems too good to be true, and that's because it is. It's one huge con.

A con man is someone who cheats people by persuading them to believe something that is not true. It has been almost one hundred years since Charles Ponzi, the namesake of the Ponzi scheme, was imprisoned. But Ponzi schemes are more prevalent today than ever before. Why? Does the mastermind behind the Ponzi scheme lie to us? Yes, but we also lie to ourselves. We know it is too good to be true, but we lie to ourselves out of laziness, greed, or some other distortion of our beautiful humanity. We fall for the world's false promises of happiness in the same way and for the same reasons.

These are just a couple of simple examples, but the world promises us happiness in a thousand ways. We give in to these false promises more easily at some times in our lives than at others. The desire for pleasure, money, possessions, success, power, and other worldly things seduces us. The bottom line, of course, is that we desire things that are not good for us. We know trading happiness for pleasure is a bad trade, but we make the trade anyway. We know that just doing what we want won't make us happy, but we want to believe it will. The lies and false promises surrounding happiness wear a thousand different masks, but they all have their roots in the modern culture's philosophy: The meaning of life is to get what you want, and the more you get of what you want, the happier you will be. And we have settled for this second-rate imitation of happiness for so long that we have become immune to these false promises and lies.

We have been lied to thousands of times throughout our lives about the very nature of happiness and how it is attained. Even in Christian circles we have ways of lying about it, saying things like, "It is selfish to think about your own happiness," or "God doesn't want you to think about your own happiness." That's not true. These are also lies. You were created for happiness. God wants you to be happy. That's an idea worth reflecting on: *God wants you to be happy*. The world tells you that God wants you to be miserable, but that's a lie. In fact, God created you for happiness. That's why human beings are at their best when they are happy.

Don't get me wrong—I am under no illusion that God wants us to be blissfully happy all the time and never experience disappointment, inconvenience, or suffering. Clearly these are all part of his plan and contribute to our quest to become the-best-version-of-ourselves. The best I can discern so far in my own life suggests that God wants us to experience happiness and even moments of unparalleled joy in this life, and then unending and blissful joy in the next life. And yet, these things are not incompatible with the inevitable suffering that we all experience in life.

I suppose it comes down to one foundational question: How long do you want to be happy for? If you just want to be happy for a couple of hours, take a nap. But I want more than that, and you do too. We yearn for long-term happiness, lasting happiness, and when it really comes down to it, that itch is a yearning for joy, which transcends simple happiness.

The good news is there is another path. You don't have to stay on the highway of lies

and the path of misery. Sooner or later we realize that what the world has to offer is simply not enough to satisfy us. It is only then that most of us turn to four of life's biggest questions:

- Who am I?
- What am I here for?
- What matters most?
- What matters least?

Our curiosity about these important questions reveals our zest for life. In each of these questions is an acknowledgment that we are each unique, that life has meaning and purpose, that life is short, and that we are pilgrims passing through this world, grasping at happiness and curious to know the answers to these questions and so much more. For many people curiosity peaks between the ages of two and three, partially as a result of being told to stop asking why. It's time to reignite your curiosity about who you are, what you are here for, what matters most, and what matters least, so that you can start living the life that you most likely imagined when you considered the questions at the end of the previous chapter. Now is the perfect time to get started.

I'VE BEEN LYING TO MYSELF

If we are going to move beyond the lies that our culture is constantly filling our hearts and minds with, we have to be equally committed to stop lying to ourselves. We don't like being lied to by other people, and yet we have an astounding capacity to deceive ourselves.

One of the reasons we accept and absorb the world's lies so easily is because we live in a culture of pretense and lies. Along with our hunger for happiness and truth, we are hungry for the authentic. We want someone, somewhere, to actually be what he or she appears to be. Even this is complex, because we project perfection onto people so easily and then act surprised when they are not perfect. The first time we do this is usually with our parents. At some point as little people we discover that our parents are just regular people.

Authentic and perfect are not the same thing. The authentic person acknowledges that he is not perfect. He is open, honest, and vulnerable about his imperfections, but he is committed to striving to overcome those imperfections and is certainly not using them as excuses to engage in self-destructive behavior or behavior that negatively impacts others.

We lie to ourselves in so many ways. I have often wondered if perhaps doing so is necessary to some extent in order to stay sane. Perhaps if the whole truth about ourselves, life, and the world were instantly revealed to us, we would have a psychotic break. Being surrounded by and accepting of so many lies for so long, it would simply be too overwhelming.

Ego and image have always played an important role in people's lives, and you and I are no different. We are intensely attached to being perceived in a positive light, even by people we don't know and will never meet—perhaps most telling, we even want to be perceived positively by people we don't like.

In short, we want *everyone* to like us. This of course leads us to present ourselves in ways that are inauthentic. This is a recipe for disaster and directly tied to one of the lessons I have learned the hard way too often, which I mentioned a few pages back: *I am never happy when I pretend to be someone I am not.*

People have always pretended to be more than who they really are. We have all done it. Driven by ego and a desire to maintain a certain image, we pretend to be more or different than who we actually are. The birth of social media has put this pretending on steroids. The tragic results of this aspect of our culture are unending. First and foremost, the obsession with social media distracts us from actually living life and embracing the present moment. It robs us of life, because it robs us of the present moment. So often in my travels around the world, I have been amazed by how obsessed so many people are with taking photos, rather than immersing themselves in the experience before them.

Today I am in Paris, and as I sit here writing, the sun is just coming up. It's a marvelous city, and of course it's filled with tourists. If I wandered down to the Louvre at any time today, I would find a massive crowd in front of da Vinci's *Mona Lisa*. Each person would be trying to take a photo, and three minutes later most of them would post their photo on their social media platform of choice. People are more interested in getting a photo than they are in actually experiencing the artistic wonder before them.

Social media robs us of life. It takes our focus off living life and shifts it to presenting a false image of ourselves and our lives to other people. As with a first date or a job interview, most people present themselves in the best possible light on social platforms. And those who don't tend to do so for other ego reasons. We seem more interested in pretending to live interesting lives than actually living interesting lives.

Last year I was forwarded the following weekly email from the principal of a high school to the students' parents.

Seeming Rather Than Being

A Latin phrase that was shared with me once has always stayed in the back of my mind: esse quam videri, which translates into "to be rather than to seem to be."

Let's acknowledge the fact that all of us are tired of people who try to be something they aren't.

I hope, in life, each of our children will work to be something they are rather than settle for seeming to be something they, in fact, are not.

While on the subject of seeming, social media platforms seem like such a waste of time to me. When our youth expose themselves to too great a degree to habits like these social platforms, they risk seeming rather than being. They are trying to present themselves as they wish to be (and wish to be seen) and in doing so are belittling some measure of their own individuality and essence, or who in fact they are. The impact on self-esteem that flows from this one sentence is disastrous.

On social media, our egos tempt us to present ourselves how we would like others to see us, rather than as we really are, and by constantly exposing ourselves to other people's mundane thoughts, we are unlikely to come up with original thoughts of our own and develop a true sense of self.

One of my greatest hopes is that we will allow (and teach) our children to be comfortable and confident being rather than succumbing to seeming as they embark on whatever journey is ahead of them.

Life is too short to waste time on social platforms. Life is too meaningful to worry about seeming when our children can and should be using that time being.

Esse quam videri.

***

Pretending is life-limiting. Social media limits our ability to actually experience life, but it is only one example of how we squander the present moment and miss out on life. Many years ago I wrote, "Sooner or later, we all rise or fall to the level of our friendships." I still believe that, though it also seems increasingly true that sooner or later, we rise or fall to the level of our social media engagement. As Christians we should see social media as a way to bring a positive message of hope to a realm filled with so much negativity and hopelessness.

So yes, the world lies to us, but we also lie to ourselves—and we lie about ourselves. Who are you pretending to be right now? What are you lying to yourself about right now?

We are really good at deceiving ourselves. Most people think they are better listeners than they are; most people think they are better drivers than they really are; most people think they are healthier than they actually are; and most of us think we are better Christians than we are.

We expect the truth from other people, but so often we dismiss that expectation for ourselves. It seems that we are afraid of the truth, but we needn't be. Truth is beautiful, and the truth about you is beautiful. You and I are not perfect, but we are beautifully imperfect. There is truth in that.

Stop pretending to be someone you are not, living a life you are not. Stop lying to yourself. And pray for me that I can stop lying and pretending too.

In all of this there is an uncomfortable question that is both essential and rarely pondered: What place are we willing to give truth in our lives? Are we willing to place truth on a throne in our lives, or do we want to hide it in the closet? Is there a connection between happiness and our relationship with truth? Could a little more truth make us a little happier; could a lot more truth make us a lot happier?

SO MANY LIES
ABOUT CHRISTIANITY

For two thousand years, non-Christians have been spreading lies about Christians and Christianity. Some of this has been done intentionally and maliciously, while most of it has probably been caused by simple ignorance. You could fill whole libraries with the lies that have been told about Christians and Christianity. The world lies about this subject more than anything else. It is therefore no surprise that in this current culture of lies, where truth is valued so little, Christianity is a constant target. In this section we will look at some of the most prominent of these lies, and why the culture clings to them so tightly.

Let's briefly explore five of the biggest lies about Christianity. My purpose here is not to provide comprehensive rebuttals to each of these lies, but to provide context for the biggest lie in the history of Christianity.

#1. JESUS DIDN'T EXIST.

If people wish to argue about whether or not Jesus rose from the dead, fair enough. If they don't believe he performed the miracles reported in the Gospels, fair enough. But whether or not Jesus existed as a particular person who lived in a particular region of the world at a specific time in history is completely beyond dispute for anybody with even an ounce of intellectual honesty.

The early Christians orally documented and passed along the events of Jesus' life and his teachings in great detail. Christian writers later recorded what Jesus' disciples had witnessed firsthand and shared with the earliest Christian communities. Beyond these, both Jewish and Roman historians wrote about Jesus—the most famous of these was Josephus. And yet, the lie that Jesus never existed is still alive and well.

Just today, I was reading what people who hate Jesus say about him, and came across this: "This Jesus is nothing but a collection of stolen myths, stolen identities, and a bunch of meaningless, worthless hypocritical and contradictory teachings. There has never been a character in all of history that is as fictitious as this Nazarene idiot. He is nothing more than a lie."

In our own times, our culture has been subtly and persistently nudging Jesus toward the same category as Santa Claus and the Easter Bunny. The idea that Jesus is nothing more than a figment of Christian imagination is both disingenuous and an outright lie. While an increasing number of people may claim that Jesus is just an idea, the reality is that he is a clearly established historical figure who has influenced human history more than any other person.

#2. THE RESURRECTION IS A MYTH.

There are very few ancient events that have greater historical certainty than Jesus' death on the cross. Three days later is when lies about Jesus and Christianity kicked into high gear. It must have been some Sunday morning, and it didn't take long for lies to start spreading about his resurrection from the dead.

The first and most common lie is that Jesus' disciples came in the night and stole his body from the tomb. Possible? Sure. Likely? Not so much. The tomb had been sealed and was guarded. Perhaps more convincing is the fact that the same Jesus of Nazareth who died on the cross after being horribly tortured appeared over the next forty days to more than five hundred people on twelve different occasions. These five hundred eyewitnesses would be more than enough to convince any modern court, but because the Resurrection is so central to the Christian faith, it will be questioned and doubted until the end of time. Now, it is possible that these five hundred people were all lying. But have you ever tried to get a few people to keep a secret? This is almost always unsuccessful. Most of the time two teenagers can't get their stories straight about where they were and what they were doing last night. Then there is the haunting reality that many people who claimed that Jesus had risen from the dead were killed for saying so. Who would die for a lie?

Finally, there is the question of the body. If Jesus didn't rise from the dead, where is the body? Someone would have had to remove it—more than one person, presumably. Imagine how difficult it would have been to keep that secret. "I know where Jesus' body is!"

#3. CHRISTIANITY PREYS ON THE WEAK AND IGNORANT.

Some horrible things have been done in the name of Christianity and by Christians, though it is essential to note that in each case the atrocities committed were a departure from Christian belief and teaching. Some doctors, lawyers, schoolteachers, and people of all beliefs have done horrible things in the name of their profession or belief. In every case, they were mistaken, wrong, and in some cases mentally ill. But we don't say that because some doctors have done horrible things, the medical profession is a lie and should be abolished from the face of the earth. It is critical that we not confuse individuals' behavior with Christianity and Christian teaching, even when the individuals are Christians.

The abuse of something good does not diminish the good itself. Some people abuse their role as parents, but that does not make parenting bad and false. Parenting is a good and beautiful thing. The abuse of something good does not diminish the good itself. Some people abuse their role as Christians, but that does not make Christianity bad or false.

Now to address this particular lie that Christianity preys on the weak and ignorant. Christianity has been the premier defender of human rights and dignity for two thousand years. Christianity has done more for the poor than any other institution in history. Christianity has been a tireless advocate for the worker, and Christianity is responsible for the education of more people than any other group in every age since Jesus rose from the dead.

The actions of Christians and Christianity in general are incongruent with this claim. If Christianity were so intent on keeping people weak and ignorant, Christians throughout the ages would not have labored so diligently to liberate billions of people from weakness and ignorance.

#4. CHRISTIANITY IS ANTI-INTELLECTUAL AND ANTI-SCIENTIFIC.

As with all things Christian, it usually helps to start with Jesus himself. He was not an elitist, but he was intellectual and astute. Everything he taught was a profound reconsideration and reconstruction of the Jewish intellectual tradition. And yet he also possessed the astounding gift of a populist—the ability to present the most complex concepts and ideas in a way that is both simple and practical. Jesus presented both the practical wisdom and supernatural mysteries of his teachings so they would be accessible to as many people as possible.

Christianity has consistently been accused of being anti-intellectual and anti-scientific, and there are some grounds for these claims. The cases of Copernicus and Galileo are most commonly cited, and there is no question that Christianity responded poorly in both cases. But it is important to note that over time Christianity has been humbled by these and other mistakes, has reexamined its role in both the intellectual and scientific fields, and has adapted.

At the same time, to accuse Christianity of being anti-intellectual is ludicrous. Universities have their origin in medieval Christian tradition. Christian cathedral schools and monastic schools were the forerunners of the university system and date back to the sixth century in many places. The rise of education, schools, and universities in particular was not continuous. World events such as war, plague, famine, and changes in political and religious power all inhibited the steady progression and expansion of the school and university systems. But what is certain is that Christianity was responsible for the growth of the university system. Furthermore, in recognizing the dignity of every human person, Christianity became the champion of education for the poor. It is also of particular note that it was Christianity that championed the case for women to have equal access to education. This can be traced all the way back to Benedict and his twin sister, Scholastica, in the fifth and sixth centuries.

To accuse Christianity of being anti-intellectual is nothing short of nonsense. I have heard the point well argued, but well-argued nonsense is still nonsense.

To accuse Christianity of being anti-scientific is also a lie. First, it is no small matter to point out that even the most famous scientists who are often described as being persecuted by Christianity were themselves committed Christians. Have there been some Christians who were anti-science? Yes. Are some Christians today anti-science? Yes. But the broad position of Christianity today is that faith and reason are compatible and in fact inseparable.

Nonetheless, society continues to heap our mistakes of the past upon all Christians in all places and all times. This is akin to blaming all Germans now and forever for Hitler's crimes against humanity. Anyone with any common sense realizes that this is simply unjust. It would also be akin to accusing Americans today of supporting slavery simply because slavery was once legal in this country.

The famous atheist Christopher Hitchens wrote, "Thanks to the telescope and the microscope, religion no longer offers an explanation of anything important." He was famous for being an atheist, but he was also famous for accusing Christians of having narrow vision. And yet, his own words seem to be the fruit of an astoundingly narrow vision.

Science discovers and describes the universe for us, and the laws of nature discovered by science outline the ordered regularities of nature. But science cannot provide deeply personal answers to your deeply personal questions. It cannot answer those four questions we identified earlier: Who are you? What are you here for? What matters most? What matters least?

It would seem to me that the tables have turned. While there were times when some Christians were anti-intellectual and anti-science, today the great majority of academics and scientists appear to be blindly anti-Christian—and even more so, unlike their forefathers, they seem to be anti-God. Perhaps a thousand years from now they will find the humility that Christianity found to reassess their position, though I hope for their sake and ours that it doesn't take that long. For it is my deeply held belief that science will do its best work when faith and reason are reunited in a vigorous pursuit of truth.

Christianity has a rich intellectual and scientific history. That history is not without blemish; no history is. And today, more than ever, Christianity celebrates the friendship and partnership of faith and reason in humanity's quest to further understand ourselves and the universe.

#5. CHRISTIANITY IS ANTI-SEX.

Christianity has long been accused of producing sexual frustrations of all types among believers by being anti-sex. Christian-bashers have expanded this into the gross generalization that Christianity is opposed to pleasure and fun of any type. Not so—

quite the opposite, in fact. It may come as a surprise to many to discover that God wants you to have an amazing sex life.

The beauty and genius of Christian sexuality is that it protects people from being objectified and used simply for another person's selfish pleasure. If you have a daughter, how would you feel about her being used by a man who did not love or care for her, simply for his own sexual gratification? My experience has been that fathers quickly unite to protect their daughters from this type of situation. God wants to protect all of his children from being objectified and used, sexually or otherwise, and he calls on all Christians and all men and women of goodwill to join him in this quest.

Human sexuality is a topic worthy of a whole book unto itself. Our sexuality is an incredibly precious and powerful gift. It stands to reason that something so precious should not be abused or squandered. Far from being anti-sex, Christianity is pro-sexuality. Sex can lead to great joy or great misery. God wants our sexuality to be the source of great joy for us.

***

From the beginning, there has been no shortage of lies about Jesus, his followers, and Christianity in general. Today is no different. Lies are always swirling around Christianity. Other common lies today include: Christians hate all non-Christians; Christians think everyone else is going to hell; smart people are not Christian; Christianity is dying and won't be around for much longer. We have barely scratched the surface here, but my point is not to cover every lie or even many of the lies.

I wanted to be clear that non-Christians have been lying about us from the very beginning of Christianity. Most of these lies are the result of ignorance, as I mentioned at the beginning of this chapter. Some are the result of intentional misinformation, and a handful are a malicious personal attack upon Jesus in an attempt to discredit the entire Christian faith. Some of these lies are aimed at our theology and beliefs, and others are aimed at the Christian way of life. The sad thing about all these lies is they have destroyed real people's chances at happiness. They have done tremendous damage to so many people, and it is important to acknowledge that. These lies have stopped millions, possibly billions of people from discovering the joy and genius of Christianity.

We also need to acknowledge and confront the uncomfortable truth that as Christians we lie to each other, to other people, and to ourselves with disturbing regularity. Non-Christians may lie about us, but we lie to ourselves. It is this fact—that we lie to ourselves—that is of particular importance here. Humanity's ability to deceive itself knows no limits.

More than anything else, I want to set the stage so that together we can explore the biggest lie in the history of Christianity. Amazingly, it is not a lie that non-Christians tell about Christians; it's a lie we tell ourselves.

Let's take a look.

THE BIGGEST LIE

The lies of this world suck the life out of us by destroying our joy. Truth breeds joy. The Gospel animates our lives with that same joy. There is plenty of evidence that the joy we seek can be found by embracing the teachings of Jesus. So what is it that holds us back from fully embracing the Gospel of Jesus Christ?

Our fear and brokenness can be an obstacle. God invites us to a total surrender and we are afraid to let go. The culture and all its distractions can prevent us from seeing the beauty of the life God invites us to live. Self-loathing, unwillingness to forgive ourselves and others, biases and prejudices that have been born from past

experiences, complacency toward others in need, selfishness—these are all real obstacles in our quest to authentically live the teachings of Jesus.

The myriad of lies that have always swirled around Christianity have sown doubt in the hearts and minds and eroded the faith of millions. But one lie is having a diabolical impact on the lives of modern Christians. It is the biggest lie in the history of Christianity. And now we have arrived at the heart of the matter. It is worth noting that this lie is not one that non-Christians tell. It's a lie we tell ourselves as Christians.

This is the lie: Holiness is not possible.

The great majority of modern Christians don't actually believe holiness is possible. Sure, we believe it is possible for our grandmothers or some medieval saint—just not for us. We don't believe holiness is possible for us. This is one of the greatest tragedies of every Christian era.

Search your heart. Do you believe holiness is possible for you? Most Christians don't believe that it is.

I am not sure when or where this belief captured its stranglehold on the spiritual life of Christians and the Church. No doubt there is a complex series of psychological reasons and excuses that cause us to accept and believe this lie. This lie is diabolical in its subtlety. There is evil genius in its effectiveness. It is awful and yet you cannot help but acknowledge its evil genius. To paralyze and neutralize almost every generation of Christians with a single idea is a brilliant feat. Diabolical and evil, but brilliant nonetheless.

It is astounding that just one lie can neutralize the majority of Christians. That's right, neutralize. This lie takes us out of the game and turns us into mere spectators in the epic story of Christianity that continues to unfold in every generation. This one lie is largely, if not primarily, responsible for ushering in the post-Christian modern era throughout Western civilization. It may be the devil's greatest triumph in modern history. This is the holocaust of Christian spirituality.

In a thousand ways every day we tell ourselves and each other that holiness is not possible. We don't use that language, but the fact that the word *holiness* has disappeared from our dialogue is proof that we consider it either irrelevant or unattainable. When is the last time you heard someone speak about holiness?

Paul was abundantly clear in 1 Thessalonians 4:3 that the very will of God is our holiness. God wants us to live holy lives, grow in character and virtue, and become the-best-version-of-ourselves.

But we are too busy with a hundred other things. We don't have time to think about holiness. The very idea of it is cast aside by many as a quest for an impossible perfection. But holiness is not about being perfect, as we will soon discover.

First, however, we have to get beyond the lie that holiness is not possible, because we cannot completely experience the joy that God wants for us—and that we want for ourselves—until we do.

The saddest part of all this is that this diabolical lie can be utterly demolished, completely debunked, in about ninety seconds. So let's talk about how we demolish this lie in our hearts, minds, souls, and church communities. This is the first step toward a full understanding of our beautiful faith. This is the first step toward reestablishing our Christian identity in society. This is the first step toward building a better world in which our children and grandchildren can grow free and strong, and so much more. This is the first step.

PROVE IT!

The lie that has convinced so many Christians that holiness isn't possible is easy to disprove. It saddens me that we don't teach and reteach every Christian how to overcome this debilitating lie. And the devastating truth is that it can be disproven in just a couple of pages. Though it would be even better if we taught every Christian that holiness is possible with such clarity, and reminded them so often, that the lie would never have a chance to take root. But the lie has deeply rooted itself in our Christian communities and in our society, so let's take a look at it.

Suppose we are having coffee together and I say to you, "Can you go out tomorrow and create just one Holy Moment?" Not a holy life or even a holy day. Not a holy hour or even a holy fifteen minutes—just one single Holy Moment.

You will probably ask, "What is a Holy Moment?"

"A Holy Moment is a moment when you open yourself to God. You make yourself available to him. You set aside what you feel like doing in that moment, and you set aside self-interest, and for one moment you simply do what you prayerfully believe God is calling you to do in that moment. That is a Holy Moment."

"I think I've got it," you say, "but tell me one more time—what is a Holy Moment?"

"Very good," I reply. "A Holy Moment is a moment when you are being the person God created you to be, and you are doing what you believe God is calling you to do in that moment. It is an instance where you set aside self-interest, personal desire, and what you feel like doing or would rather be doing, and embrace what you believe will bring the most good to the most people in that moment."

"OK, I've got it," you confirm, and so I ask again, "Can you go out tomorrow, collaborate with God in this way, and create one Holy Moment?"

Sure you can. It's not overwhelming. It's not confusing. It doesn't require a massive intellect, a doctorate in theology, or even a rare grasp of theology. It is accessible, achievable, and immensely practical.

This is a thing of beauty. The first line of John Keats' poem *Endymion* reads: "A thing of beauty is a joy forever." A Holy Moment is a thing of beauty. The poem continues, "Its loveliness increases; it will never pass into nothingness." This idea that we are discussing, this approach to collaborating with God to create Holy Moments, is a thing of beauty for two reasons. The first reason is that what we have just discussed in the last three hundred words proves that *HOLINESS IS POSSIBLE FOR YOU.* God loves collaborating with humanity, and if you can collaborate with God and create just one single Holy Moment, that alone proves that holiness is possible for you.

The heroes, champions, and saints who have exemplified Christian living for two thousand years did not live holy lives. It is a mistake to step back and look at their lives and say, "She lived a holy life" or "He lived a truly holy life." And these men and women that we place on pedestals would be the first to admit that they did not live holy lives—they lived Holy Moments. Their lives were not a single action. Rather, they lived life like you and I, one moment at a time. Did they collaborate with God to create Holy Moments? Yes. Did they turn their backs on God at other times and create unholy moments? Absolutely. In fact, it is essential to note that between all the Holy Moments these champions of Christianity were creating with God, they did some really sick, crazy, dark, twisted, demented, and messed-up stuff. Take Paul the Apostle as an example. We are talking about a guy who hunted down Christians to murder them. If he didn't murder them himself, he was certainly complicit and gave the orders to have them imprisoned, tortured, and murdered. I don't know about you, but this gives me great hope.

How did Paul overcome this horrible legacy? First, he had a remarkable encounter with Jesus when he was knocked from his horse. This encounter created an incredible joy and a profound awareness of who Jesus was and what he had transformed in Paul's life. He then wanted as many people as possible to encounter Jesus and develop this profound awareness of him as Paul had himself.

This is why Paul dedicated himself to a great collaboration with God and set out each morning to create Holy Moments by living a life of Christian character, values, and virtue. He collaborated so powerfully with God, created so many Holy Moments, and taught so many others to do the same, that most people don't even think about the dark and twisted things I mentioned above when people speak about Paul.

This idea of the Holy Moment is a thing of beauty, and as John Keats points out: "A thing of beauty is a joy forever: Its loveliness increases; it will never pass into nothingness." Every good act, every collaboration with God, every Holy Moment fueled by grace echoes throughout history. The good we do is never lost, it never ends, and it never dies. In other places, in other times, in other people, the good we do lives on forever. That is why Holy Moments, however small, however seemingly insignificant, are so powerful. They change people's lives, and collectively they change the whole course of human history. One single Holy Moment is a thing of beauty. Its loveliness increases. It will never pass into nothingness.

But I said there were two reasons why this concept of the Holy Moment is a thing of beauty. The second reason is that it is replicable. You don't need to read another book to learn how to collaborate with God and create the second Holy Moment. The fact that you can cooperate with God to create one Holy Moment proves that holiness is possible for you, and it provides the blueprint for thousands of Holy Moments.

The truly beautiful thing is that this idea can be replicated an infinite number of times. If you can do it once, you can do it twice. We don't need to have coffee again next week before you can create your second Holy Moment. You only need to learn the lesson of the Holy Moment once. From now on, you can apply it as many times as you commit to.

If you can create just one Holy Moment next Monday, you can create two on Tuesday and four on Wednesday, eight on Thursday, and so on. There is no limit to the number of Holy Moments you can create, other than your desire and the consciousness to grasp each moment for God as it is unfolding.

Some people will ask genuinely, "How do I know what God wants me to do in any given moment?" This is a great question. We discussed earlier that God wants us to live holy lives, grow in character and virtue, and become the-best-version-of-ourselves. These three things are interconnected. You cannot grow in character and virtue and not become a-better-version-of-yourself, and vice versa. You cannot become a-better-version-of-yourself and not draw one step closer to God. And every time you grow in character and become a-better-version-of-yourself, you are living a Holy Moment.

The first thing to be clear about is that our mere openness to doing the will of God is pleasing to him—as are our efforts to discern what God is inviting us to do and experience in any given moment. And perhaps most important, we will get better at this as we continue to practice it. Even though we may fumble around and make many mistakes, each effort to know and do God's will attunes us ever more closely to the promptings of the Holy Spirit. In our first attempts to seek and do what God is calling us to do in any given moment, we may hear only the faintest whisper. And this whisper will be competing with the many other voices we hear each time we have a decision to make. But over time, as we collaborate with God to create more and more Holy Moments, the whisper will grow louder and clearer.

It may also be helpful to have litmus test questions, such as: Will this help me become a-better-version-of-myself? Will this help me grow in character and virtue? Does this contradict Jesus' teachings? Will this action bring harm to another person? Will this help or prevent others from becoming a-better-version-of-themselves? And if we find ourselves confused, it is best to turn that confusion or lack of clarity into an opportunity for prayer, by turning to God in our hearts and asking, "Lord, what is it that you want most for me and from me in this moment?"

It is also important to note that we need God's grace to create Holy Moments. We can't do this alone. This is not a self-empowerment thing. Holy Moments are created with God's grace. The good news is that God is generous with grace and will never deny you the grace you need to create Holy Moments. It is never God's grace that is lacking, but rather our willingness to cooperate with his grace.

When I say the word *grace*, what other word comes to mind? *Amazing*. Grace is amazing. We need God's amazing grace. We need it badly and we need it now. Time is short, but he knows that, and I am excited to see God unleash a whole bunch of amazing grace in your life and mine, in your family and mine, in your neighborhood and mine, in your country and mine, and in our world.

Amazing grace. We have all been blind and stupid at times. We have been cowards and lovers of comfort. We have been blind and lost, but all that is about to change because amazing grace is going to open our eyes so that we can see what is really happening within us and around us.

The world needs changing, and this single idea of Holy Moments can change the world again. It has before.

The world needs changing, and the truth is, it will not likely change for the better unless this change is led by Christians. No group of people is in a better position to change the world than Christians, but we need to get our act together; we need to get organized, unified, and mobilized.

What is it that the world needs? Holy Moments.

Your marriage needs Holy Moments. This is what your children, friends, neighbors, and work colleagues need. Your school, business, and church all need Holy Moments.

This simple and beautiful idea is central to the Christian life, despite the fact that we have lost sight of it or abandoned it, or both. It is accessible to all men, women, and children, and it doesn't require a towering intellect. Rich and poor, educated and uneducated, single and

married—everyone can understand this uncomplicated approach to transforming the simple moments of our everyday lives into moments that transform us and other people and bring about a better world where our children and grandchildren can grow free and strong.

So, get out there and start creating some Holy Moments.

ONE BEAUTIFUL TRUTH

Truth is beautiful. Despite the title, this book is not about lies. It is about truth—in particular, the one central truth that encapsulates the joy of Christian living. The truth that Holy Moments are possible reminds us that in the face of the overwhelming problems in our world, we can wake each day and joyfully share God's truth, goodness, and beauty with everyone who crosses our path.

The modern world is a complex world, and the problems our world faces are complex problems. So the temptation is to turn to complexity for answers to these complex problems. But the answer is not more complexity, and the solutions to our complex problems are much simpler than we seem willing to realize. We have become hypnotized by complexity, but the essence of Christianity is simple. In that simplicity, Christianity is good and beautiful, positive and hopeful. Goodness, beauty, and hope— these are things that people need. They are things that I need. And if you and I don't allow these things to flow through us into the world, then who will? When will they? And can the world and all the people trapped in misery wait? I think not. I think now is the time. Now is *our* time.

Can one truth change the world? I believe it can. Is it possible for just one beautiful truth to change your life? I know with absolute certainty that this is possible. How can I be so very sure? I have seen it happen before. And I've experienced it. The single truth that Holy Moments are possible and that you and I—with all our faults and flaws, defects and weaknesses, brokenness and constant need—can collaborate with God and create a single Holy Moment is life-changing.

It was this single beautiful truth that completely changed my life when I was about fifteen years old. Since then I have been fumbling around trying to cooperate and collaborate with God to create Holy Moments. Some days have been successful; other days have been complete failures warped by selfishness and worldly desire. There have been some marvelous moments over the years when I have known without a doubt that the hand of God was on my shoulder, guiding and encouraging me. There have also been some desperately sad moments when I felt more alone than I ever thought possible, when I curled into a fetal position and cried out to God but got no answer. But by some grace I got back up, literally and figuratively, and pressed on. Sometimes it took hours, sometimes it took days, and I am ashamed that sometimes it took weeks or months. But sooner or later, I am always led back to this singular truth that Holy Moments are possible.

In a world that can seem so dark at times, God gives you and me a candle and a match and says, "You are the light of the world." You? Me? I know, it seems impossible, but it is both the story of Christianity and the legacy of each Christian. And yet, all these words can feel like little more than a theory. So, let's talk about the beautiful truth that Holy Moments are possible in practical terms. Let's make it real and bring it to life with everyday examples that we can all relate to.

***

John Miller discovered that his neighbor three houses down had broken his leg. He had never met this neighbor, but on Saturday when he was mowing his lawn he noticed the lawn three houses down was getting a little long. So when he was finished mowing his own lawn that Saturday afternoon, he went down and mowed his neighbor's lawn. That was a Holy Moment. John mowed his neighbor's lawn every Saturday for eight weeks.

***

Lillian Lopez thought she was going to lose her mind over her teenage daughter's attitude and behavior. She had prayed for months asking God to do something, but it turned out God wanted Lillian to do something. The following Sunday morning, she woke her daughter at 7:00 a.m., saying, "Get yourself ready; we are leaving in twenty minutes." As you can imagine, that wasn't too well received. "Where are we going?" her daughter yelled. "I'll tell you on the way," her mother replied. Earlier in the week Lillian had bought two leather-bound journals. They weren't expensive, but money was tight and so they didn't come without sacrifice. Lillian took her daughter to their favorite breakfast spot. After they had ordered, she pushed one of the journals across the table. "What's this?" her daughter asked. "It's the book of your life," Lillian answered. "A place to write your hopes and dreams, a place to plan, and somewhere to doodle when doodling is what best helps you think about your future." Her daughter's eyes began to fill with tears. It was a Holy Moment. "So, what are your dreams?" Lillian asked her daughter. They talked for almost an hour about her daughter's hopes and dreams for her life, and she started writing them in her journal. Then she noticed that there was a second journal on her mother's side of the table, in the corner. "What's the other journal?" she asked her mom. That was another Holy Moment. "That's my book of life," Lillian replied. "I figure it's time for me to start dreaming again."

***

Emmanuel wasn't young, but he wasn't old. At fifty and in good health, he hoped he had a lot of life still ahead of him. He had some extra vacation time, so he decided to have a staycation: a week off at home, just resting, getting organized, having breakfast with his wife instead of rushing out the door to work, driving his kids to school, and picking them up each day. It turned out to be a whole week of Holy Moments. Each day when he got home from dropping the kids at school, he would take a walk. Two blocks from where he lived was a retirement home. He drove by it on the way to work every day, but never really gave it much thought. But a couple of Sundays past he had read an article about how the average resident in a retirement home gets fewer than one visitor a month. So, on Tuesday as he was walking past, he decided to stop in. The truth is, he had to force himself to do it. But he pushed through his discomfort, walked in, and approached the front desk. It was an awkward moment, he told me, standing there at the reception desk. "I live down the road and I have a bit of extra time today, so I was wondering if you have any residents who don't get many visitors. I was thinking I could visit with a couple and that might brighten their day a little," Emmanuel explained to the receptionist. "That is very thoughtful," she said. "I know just the person." Then she pointed down a hallway that must have had seventy or eighty doors, and said, "Walk down that hallway, pick any room, knock on the door, and you will be in the right room." Emmanuel smiled uncomfortably and walked down the hallway. Because his birthday was the twenty-first of January, he picked room number twenty-one, knocked on the door, and after hearing a rather grumpy "Come in!" he went in. Sitting in the corner was a gentleman by the name of William Butler. Emmanuel introduced himself and they began to talk. Bill was a fascinating guy. They talked about life and family, business and God. It was a Holy Moment—ten years ago. Today, Emmanuel and Bill are best friends.

***

Joan Binzer worked at a greeting card company. Less than three miles from the company was a prison with four hundred male occupants, the worst of the worst offenders. Joan had worked at the greeting card company for thirteen years, and almost every morning as she drove past the prison on the way to work, she wondered about the prisoners and what had gone wrong. As a mother, she couldn't help but think how hard it must be for their mothers. As May came around that year, Joan had an idea. She went to her boss and said, "What if for our community service project this quarter, we take some Mother's Day cards and stamps over to the prison for the prisoners to send to their moms?" Joan's boss said he would check with the prison and get back to her. The following week he told Joan the prison warden was very appreciative and supportive. The next week, Joan and nine of her colleagues went over to the prison with two hundred Mother's Day cards, thinking that not all the prisoners would necessarily want to participate. It quickly became apparent that her assumption was completely wrong. Before Joan had helped a dozen prisoners pick a card for their mothers, she had been asked seven times, "Would it be OK if I took two?" Joan finally worked up the nerve to ask one of the prisoners, "What is your name, sir?" "Jimmy Johnson, ma'am!" he replied. "Why do you want two, Jimmy?" Joan asked. "Well, my mom did the best she could but she had her own problems, and so I was mostly raised by my grandmother. So, I was thinking if it was OK with you good people, I would send one to my grandmother too!" Joan had to use all her strength not to burst into tears. There were four hundred inmates in the prison that day, and every single one wrote a Mother's Day card. That's four hundred Holy Moments. In fact, Joan and her company ended up mailing 657 Mother's Day cards for the inmates. That's 1,057 Holy Moments.

***

Martin Coster picks up seventy-eight-year-old Michael Williams every Wednesday night and drives him to Bible study. That's a Holy Moment.

***

When Mary Wright goes through the drive-through each morning to get her coffee, she pays for the person behind her. She does it every day. When I asked her why, she replied, "So many reasons, I guess. We need to look out for each other. Lots of people have been generous to me throughout my life in large ways and small. People need to know that there are generous, thoughtful people in the world. And ultimately, I believe that thoughtfulness and generosity are contagious and can change the world." That's one of Mary's daily Holy Moments. And she's right—Holy Moments are contagious.

***

Tony Harris has discovered something about himself over the years: He is a very impatient listener. He constantly finds himself wanting to jump in, interrupt, and make a point. For four years, three times a day, he has been trying to consciously stop himself from doing this. That's a lot of patient Holy Moments. "Just by focusing on changing this one horrible habit I developed over my life, I find I am more patient with my wife, my children, my colleagues at work, my pastor, and the strangers who cross my path and, to be honest, really irritate me." Holy Moments cannot be contained; they reach out into every relationship and aspect of our lives.

***

Anastasia Petrov is a Russian immigrant and a nurse. "I love America," she says to me with her sixty-two-year-old smile. A few years ago one of the other nurses she works with at the hospital got cancer and had to take some time off work. Anastasia didn't know her very well, but she knew that the other nurse had three kids and that she needed to work. The hospital's policy allowed for the sick nurse to have six weeks off with pay, but after that her time away from work was without pay. At lunch one day Anastasia heard some of the other nurses talking about doing one of those online funding projects to help out. "We can do better than that!" Anastasia said to her colleagues. They all turned and stared at her; you see, Anastasia was a quiet woman. She was a listener. Plenty of lunch breaks would pass without her saying a single word. Perhaps it was just her personality, or perhaps it was the result of being raised in Soviet Russia. "What do you mean?" one of her colleagues finally asked her. "Everyone loves Jane [the sick nurse]. She is always doing kind things for people. We all have three twelve-hour shifts a week; all we need to do is find three nurses to volunteer an extra shift each week and Jane can keep getting paid until she is well and can come back to work." The other nurses stared at her with astonishment and admiration. "I'll organize the schedule," Anastasia added. And so she did. Each week while Jane was out of work, Anastasia found three nurses to do an extra shift so that Jane could continue to be paid her full salary. I learned about this from Sophia, another nurse at the hospital. "How long was Jane off work?" I asked Sophia. "Three years!" she replied with a smile. "Anastasia is a saint," she continued. Talk about Holy Moments. I figure Anastasia triggered about ten million Holy Moments at lunch that day.

***

There are some amazing stories here, but I don't want to give you the impression that every Holy Moment has to be huge and heroic. Holy Moments come in all shapes and sizes, but the great majority of them are small and anonymous.

- Begin each day with a short prayer of gratitude thanking God for giving you another day of life. That's a Holy Moment.
- Go out of your way to do something for your spouse that you would rather not do, as an intentional act of love. That's a Holy Moment.
- Offer the least enjoyable task of your day to God as a prayer for someone who is suffering. That's a Holy Moment.
- Control your temper, even if you are fully justified in losing it. That's a Holy Moment.
- Before making a decision, ask, "What will help me become a-better-version-of-myself?" That's a Holy Moment.
- Encourage someone, coach someone, praise someone, affirm someone. These are all Holy Moments.
- Be patient with that person who drives you crazy. That's a Holy Moment.

- Do someone else's chores. That's a Holy Moment.
- Teach someone how to pray. That's a Holy Moment.
- Give someone a life-changing book. That's a Holy Moment.
- Ask God to lead and guide you. That's a Holy Moment.
- Tell someone your faith story. That's a Holy Moment.
- Stay calm in the midst of a crisis. That's a Holy Moment.
- Choose the-best-version-of-yourself, even when you don't feel like it. That's a Holy Moment.
- Make a healthy eating choice. That's a Holy Moment.
- Recycle. That's a Holy Moment.
- Get honest with yourself about your self-destructive habits. That's a Holy Moment.
- Tell God you trust he has a great plan for you and your life. That's a Holy Moment.
- Give whoever is in front of you your full attention. That's a Holy Moment.

***

Holy Moments are possible. Holiness is possible. This is a beautiful truth, and truth animates us. This is also the very will of God. In 1 Thessalonians 4:3, we read, "This is the will of God, that you be holy." Don't let yourself be neutralized by the biggest lie in the history of Christianity. Reject that lie every day, and embrace every Holy Moment that comes your way.

But first let's have a moment of raw, unfiltered honesty. Truth is beautiful, but it can also be inconvenient, uncomfortable, and even disturbing. So, let me ask you a question: Before now, did you ever believe holiness was possible for you?

If your answer is no, I am so excited for what is ahead for you. Holiness is possible for you. This single profound, beautiful truth will change your life forever. So, let's pray together, right now: "Lord, please, I beg you, never let me forget that holiness is possible, and give me the grace and courage to go out into the world and create with you as many Holy Moments as possible. Amen."

Opportunities to create Holy Moments are everywhere. In fact, every moment is an opportunity for holiness. Learning to grasp these opportunities one moment at a time is central to the Christian life.

Holiness is possible. This is the good news that Christians everywhere need to be convinced and reminded of. This is the good news that will raise us out of our neutralized, passive, inactive state and open our hearts, minds, and souls to an amazing new reality. This single beautiful truth transforms us into people of possibility.

Part of this new reality is the joy that comes from Gospel living. The lie that holiness is not possible keeps us from the joy that God wants us to experience. You don't need to work hard at creating Holy Moments for months or years before you start to experience this joy; it is immediate. Each Holy Moment brings with it an injection of joy. Each Holy Moment is its own reward.

Holiness is possible for you! You can collaborate with God to create Holy Moments. Try it today. In the process you will become a-better-version-of-yourself, help others become a-better-version-of-themselves, and make the world a better place. Don't waste another moment—remind yourself over and over again that it is possible. Modern culture says holiness is not possible. It's a lie. If you can create one Holy Moment, that proves holiness is possible for you. Modern culture has robbed billions of people of happiness by discouraging them in their Christianity and convincing them of this single lie that holiness is not possible. But today is a day of liberation. Today I hope you have been liberated from that lie and as a result the whole world looks different.

Holiness is possible for you. This beautiful truth is the opposite of the diabolical neutralizing lie that has paralyzed so many Christians and their communities. It should be no surprise that one of the greatest truths in the history of Christianity is the exact opposite of the biggest lie in the history of Christianity. Holiness is possible, one moment at a time. This single beautiful truth can change your life forever, beginning today, beginning right now.

But it goes so far beyond you and your church community. Let's take a look at how this one idea changed the world two thousand years ago, and how it can change the world again in our times.

THE WORLD NEEDS CHANGING

Everybody knows the world needs changing. Parents are concerned about the world their children are growing up in. Grandparents often tell me they try not to think too much about the world their grandchildren will grow up in because it makes them too anxious.

I don't know anybody who thinks the world is in great shape. I don't know anyone who thinks our culture is moving in a promising direction that will be good for all men, women, and children. It seems universally understood that the world needs changing.

The primary problem concerning Christianity's role in changing the modern world is that most Christians no longer believe we are capable of accomplishing that change. This is a direct result of the fact that Christians by and large don't believe that holiness is possible. But it is also deeply connected to a false belief widely held by Christians that the culture has become so powerful that we are simply incapable of transforming it. This leads to conversations that the culture has pushed the envelope too far and the only solution is the Second Coming of Jesus Christ. This is tragic defeatism, which is the antithesis of the spirit of Christianity and at the same time an astounding form of spiritual laziness. It is nothing more than the fruit of the biggest lie in the history of Christianity. It is only because we have been deceived into believing holiness is not possible that we would believe the culture is too negative and too strong to be transformed by Christianity.

The world needs to be transformed, and nobody is in a better position to do that than Christians. In fact, I would argue that if Christians do not change the world, it will not change for the better.

The everyday Holy Moments of ordinary people like you and me is what will change the world again. I say "again" because our ancestors in faith, the first Christians, already changed the world once. The culture they had to overcome and transform was even more brutal than today's. By transforming it, the first Christians created a blueprint for cultural transformation that every generation of Christians should closely consult. But the essence of that blueprint is the idea that holiness is possible.

What I am about to say is no exaggeration. The future of Christianity and the world will rise or fall based upon the unconsidered possibility that the average person in the street is capable of collaborating with God to create Holy Moments on a daily basis.

Whenever and wherever Christians have taken the idea that holiness is possible seriously, Christianity has thrived. Whenever and wherever the biggest lie in the history of Christianity has prevailed and everyday holiness has been set aside, Christianity has fumbled along clumsily with limited impact or become stagnant. For example, in Europe today, worse than having limited impact or stagnating, we are now witnessing Christianity retreating from the culture.

The single idea that holiness is possible, effectively communicated to Christians of all ages and activated on a massive scale, is enough to turn the tide for Christianity in our society.

At the same time, Christianity needs a serious image overhaul in modern societies around the world. Too many people have accepted too many of the lies that have prevailed in society. The result is that Christianity is seen at best as a thing of the past that is no longer relevant in the modern world and at worst as a very negative influence.

So, it is going to take a brilliant strategic effort to place Christianity back at the center of modern culture. But the most brilliant strategies are usually simple, and the simplicity at the center of whatever strategy we can all agree to adopt will be Holy Moments. It is not impossible to reestablish a vibrant identity for Christianity in modern society, but it will require the grace-filled humility, cooperation, and discipline of every Christian—and especially our leaders.

Now let's return to the opening point of this chapter. Everybody knows the world needs changing. We may disagree with our non-Christian sisters and brothers about what changes are needed, but the need for change itself is indisputable. And so, the key to repositioning Christianity as an incredibly positive and powerful force in our culture is what I like to call a 100 percent issue. A 100 percent issue is one that no reasonable, rational man or woman of goodwill can disagree with. For example, I believe no child in the United States should go to bed hungry. That's a 100 percent issue.

(I do, of course, believe that no child anywhere in the world should go to bed hungry, but let's start with the United States, and stick with it as our example.)

If I said no American should go to bed hungry at night, it would no longer be a 100 percent issue. Some people would argue that many of the hungry and homeless are lazy, are voluntarily abusing substances, and have chosen the lifestyle they are living. They may be right. I don't know. It doesn't matter right now, because while some people may disagree about every American, *everyone agrees that no American child should go to bed hungry.* This is a 100 percent issue, which means nobody can disagree with you without looking foolish at the very least.

The world needs changing, and no group of people is in a better position to change the world than Christians, but we need an image overhaul. The quickest way to accomplish that would be to put ourselves on the right side of a 100 percent issue, champion that issue, and conquer it. The beautiful thing is that we wouldn't have to pretend or lie in order to do so, because it is at the core of who we are. Many politicians are always looking for the 60/40 issue and then looking to put themselves on the 60 percent side, regardless of what they believe to be good, true, right, and just.

If we came together as Christians, united as one force, regardless of our denominations or theological differences, and said, "Over the next ten years we are going to end child hunger in America," we could do it. We would need to set aside our denominational and theological differences, but surely whatever those differences are, we can all agree that Jesus doesn't want any child in the United States going to bed hungry tonight. We could do this. Christians could get this done. In fact, we are probably the only group who could.

Politicians have been trying for decades to end childhood hunger in this country and failing miserably. One in five American children go to bed hungry each night. How is that acceptable to anyone, regardless of religious creed or political affiliation? It isn't. It's a 100 percent issue.

As Christians we would lead the charge, and the social and political pressure for every other group in the country to join us in the effort would be overwhelming and undeniable. Even groups, like Fortune 500 companies and the United Way, that increasingly shy away from supporting faith-based initiatives would be under tremendous pressure to participate.

We would end childhood hunger in America. Let me say that one more time so you can let it sink in: We would end childhood hunger in America.

In the process we could completely change the image of Christianity in this country and around the world. We would no longer be seen as a massively divided people who mostly *talk about* doing good things; we would be seen as modern leaders committed to changing the world one problem at a time.

The other advantage is that we would learn Christian unity. We will not accomplish this by talking about it. We will not achieve it by debating theological differences. Christian unity will be achieved by practicing Christian unity, by spending time together and working side by side to make the world a better place. And hear me when I say this: The future of Christianity around the world depends on this unity. It is no longer just a nice idea; it is the moral imperative upon which the future of Christianity depends. The very existence of Christianity will be threatened in our lifetimes.

Everybody knows the world needs changing. Our problems internally and the challenges we face externally in society are significant. There is not a moment to waste. Holy Moments are the solution. Can one idea change the world? Yes, and this is that idea. Holiness is possible for you. Convince just 20 percent of American Christians of this single concept, engage them in the daily practice of Holy Moments, and within twelve months we would live in a very different country and culture.

Is the world a bit of a mess? Yes. Do many people see the outlook as grim? Yes. Should we as Christians see the outlook as grim? Absolutely not! Christians are people of hope, people of possibilities. So have courage, my friends, and together, let's set out to change the world as the first Christians did.

The world needs changing, yes or yes? And nobody is more capable of transforming the world for the better than Christians. Holy Moments, my brothers and sisters, are what the world needs. There is nothing happening in the world today that Christians collaborating with God to create Holy Moments cannot overcome. If we dedicate ourselves to this way of life, humanity's future will be bright.

***

Everybody loves a comeback. Everybody loves an underdog. Christianity is now that underdog, but everybody doesn't love it. It is, however, time for a Christian comeback.

The world has written us off. Lots of our own Christian brothers and sisters have given up on us. But I have not given up. Not even close. And not only have I not given up, I can see the path back. The road is before us. It is not an easy road, but the future of humanity hangs in the balance. We can stay here, bickering among ourselves about things that will mean just about nothing to just about nobody a hundred years from now, while our enemies take over the world. Or we can heal and unite as Christians and fight our way back into the light one moment at a time. History is made one moment at a time. Each moment is a moment of light or a moment of darkness, a Christian moment or an un-Christian moment, a Holy Moment or an unholy moment. I can't make you do it, but I will walk alongside you and encourage you, and I ask you to walk alongside me and encourage me, because that's what Christian brothers and sisters have been doing for two thousand years, and that is what it means to be a community of Christians.

Our enemies are trying to wipe us off the face of the earth, literally. Our enemies are not at the gates; they are inside the gates. The enemies of Christianity are trying to ensure that Christianity has no future. Will you let them do that? How will we stop them? I'm not exactly sure, but I do know this. Either we will heal or we will die. Either we will unite as Christians despite our differences, or our enemies will win and our grandchildren and their grandchildren will live in a truly post-Christian world. Let us all pray for Christian unity because it is the key to our survival. It is time we all started praying for and working toward Christian unity. There is simply too much at stake.

You may think this is just rhetoric or that I am exaggerating to prove a point. Don't let yourself be deceived. This is neither premature rhetoric nor exaggeration. This is happening right now, in our lifetime. We can bury our heads in the sand, or we can stand united and decide to do something about it.

There is an expression: turning in one's grave. It means that the dead would be disgusted at what is happening and unable to rest in peace. I know what the founding fathers of this great nation would do if they weren't turning in their graves right now, disgusted that we have let it get this far. I know what they would do if they could rise up for just one day, week, month, or year. I think you know too. But they cannot. Or can they? I think they can. I think the founding fathers can rise up and fill you and me with their courage and character so that we can stand up and say, "Enough is enough. The nonsense has gone on for far too long, and it has gone far too far." The founding fathers had their moment, and in that moment they ensured that this nation would be one of religious liberty. Our religious liberty as Christians is now being threatened like never before, and the risk is much greater than the average person on the street is aware.

Christians have a choice to make. Will we sit idly by and let this happen, or will we do everything in our power to ensure that followers of Jesus Christ are free to live his teachings for generations to come? This choice is ours.

At the same time it is essential that we resist the temptation to seek worldly solutions to spiritual problems. We should involve ourselves rigorously in the political process, but our main focus needs to remain on spiritual transformation. Holy Moments are the answer. The world needs Holy Moments.

The world will change. It always has. The question is: Will it change for the better? You and I, one moment at a time, get to answer that question together. So, let's get out there and start creating Holy Moments.

IT'S BEEN DONE BEFORE

The hardest things to do are those that have never been done before. If something has been done before, in most cases you have access to a wealth of knowledge about the best way to approach the task at hand. You can learn from someone else's mistakes and benefit from their trial and error. It is much harder to do something that has never been done before because you have no guide, no research, no map, and no expert to show you the way or point you in the right direction.

In the corporate world we talk about this idea with phrases like "hunger for best practices" and "commitment to continuous improvement." These are not modern business concepts. Christians have been practicing

these concepts for almost two thousand years.

Take as an example a twenty-first-century biblical scholar. She doesn't start from scratch, with a blank sheet of paper and a Bible. Modern biblical scholars stand on the shoulders of the giants who have gone before them. They begin by studying the discoveries of the great biblical scholars in history.

In its most basic form, think of it this way: Biblical scholar A studied the Word of God for fifty years and was widely considered the most influential biblical scholar of his time. Biblical scholar B was born thirty years before biblical scholar A died, and she began studying the Bible at an intellectual level the year A died. Is biblical scholar B going to start from the very beginning, where A started fifty years ago? I sure hope not. I hope she stands on the shoulders of A and all the best biblical scholars from the past, learns all she can about what he learned as quickly as possible, so that she can advance the Christian community even further in its collective understanding of the genius of God's Word.

That is hunger for best practices and commitment to continuous improvement, and Christians were practicing these concepts hundreds of years before they were ever mentioned in the context of business.

Do we have challenges before us? Yes, huge challenges. Are they original challenges that have never been overcome before? No. The first Christians, our ancient ancestors, dealt with very similar situations, but the scenarios they faced were even worse than those we face today. The first Christians were giants in this sense, and we are going to stand on their shoulders to learn from them by igniting our hunger for best practices and our commitment to continuous improvement. What they learned will allow us to respond to the challenges that face Christianity and society today better than ever before.

It's been done before, and that, my friends, is another thing of beauty, because by transforming their culture and changing the world, the early Christians left us a blueprint. We are going to use that blueprint to do it again.

Now, I hear someone saying, "But the culture is so much more powerful today, so the task before us is infinitely more difficult than it was for the first Christians." Maybe. I always like to stay open to the idea that I might be wrong. I find it healthy, because it helps me to grow, learn, and develop stronger bonds with my Christian and non-Christian friends.

Will it be easier or harder for us to transform the culture and change the world than it was for the first Christians? Easier, I think. I hear someone asking why, and that's good; childlike curiosity is a beautiful thing. I believe that if we can muster the same conviction and commitment as the first Christians did, it will be easier. Why? Three reasons:

1. We have legal rights that the first Christians did not.
2. There are more of us.
3. We have the technology that has been used so powerfully against Christianity, and we can harness it now for God and goodness.

So, where do we start? We begin by exploring the strategy that made the first Christians phenomenally successful. Now, it is important to acknowledge that it is unlikely the first Christians held strategic planning sessions. The Holy Spirit was moving powerfully within them. Does that mean we shouldn't develop a really well-thought-out strategy? No. Does that mean the Holy Spirit won't work powerfully in and through us? No.

Looking back, the strategy of the first Christians seems to have been very simple. Game changers usually are. In order to cut through the complexity and bureaucracy and gain broad adoption, game changers need to be ridiculously simple. Complicated strategies are incapable of gaining broad acceptance and massive adoption. The beauty of the Holy Moment is that it is staggeringly simple.

What was the strategy of the first Christians? They lived differently, they worked differently, and they loved differently than everyone else around them. It is important to understand that this most likely happened organically. The first Christians probably didn't set out to create this dynamic, but by living, working, and loving differently, they differentiated themselves in very powerful and attractive ways.

The power of contrast was one of early Christianity's best friends. First century culture was brutal. Beyond the elite who held all the power, people were treated as objects whose main purpose was to serve the needs of the Roman Empire, whatever they might be. This cold, harsh, brutal, and deeply impersonal culture actually created the perfect opportunity for Christianity to shine and rise by contrast.

In contrast to the brutal culture of the first century, Christianity and the first Christians were warm, inviting, kind, and generous, and early Christian culture was deeply personal. In a word: Christianity was attractive. The first Christians intrigued the people of their time with their selflessness in the midst of a culture where everybody seemed solely preoccupied with self-interest. That a Christian would set aside his or her self-interest to help even strangers and slaves was both baffling and appealing. The first Christians captured the imagination of their age with their love. They took seriously Jesus' directive that his disciples would be known by their love for one another and their love for others.

The first century was also dominated by a very strict hierarchical system, which created massive inequality, while in the earliest Christian communities every member held equal standing. Even the lowliest slave was given dignity and status equal to that of the wealthiest member of the Christian community. And when communities strayed from this unity and equality, Paul was quick to call them on it (see 1 Corinthians 11:18–22).

The squalor of those times also made sickness common and even the simplest infection could be life-threatening. This often led to the complete destruction of a family. Many who became sick and could not work simply died. If a family's provider died and he had sons of working age, the sons may have been able to provide at some minimal level for the family. But all too often wives and daughters were forced to sell themselves as prostitutes simply to survive.

Belonging to the Christian community was in many ways the first nonfamily form of a social net. Christian communities took care of the sick, nursing them back to health and providing for their families until the sick had recovered and were able to return to work. In turn, those who had benefited from this extraordinary love and support would pass along similar love and devotion to others in need.

Holy Moments have been a daily part of the Christian life from the very beginning.

The idea of belonging to a community that watched out for each other was also very attractive compared to the constant anxiety of everyone fending for him- or herself. This mutual social support was astoundingly attractive to the people of the early centuries of

Christianity. It fell into the category of what today we would call "too good to be true." But it was true and real and open to all men, women, and children, regardless of their social or financial status in the broader community.

But it wasn't all positive. By becoming Christians, first-century Romans and others were opening themselves to social estrangement, hostility from neighbors, and possible persecution.

It would also be a mistake to overly spiritualize the success of Christianity in its earliest form, during the first hundred years. While early Christianity was deeply rooted in the life, death, resurrection, and teachings of Jesus Christ, its success goes far beyond Jesus' unique spiritual teachings. Keep in mind early Christians had no Bibles and no churches—but they had each other.

The important piece that we need to be abundantly clear about is that the first Christians clearly differentiated themselves from the dominant culture of their times. Modern Christians blend in, and that needs to change if we are going to establish a new, vibrant, and positive identity in the midst of a culture that is proactively hostile toward Christianity.

How do we do that? By inspiring every person and every environment we touch with Holy Moments. It's time for Christians to astound the world with our generosity, kindness, patience, courage, thoughtfulness, and selfless care for the weak, poor, and forgotten.

It's time to wake up. Too often we sleepwalk through life individually, but as Christians it seems we have fallen asleep collectively. It's time for us to wake up. The enemy is not at the gates. The enemy is inside the gates.

Christianity is being attacked by secularism and intolerance, and many other forces who would like to see Christianity wiped off the face of the earth. But even in the midst of these very well-organized and -executed attacks upon our Christian faith, there are some aspects of Christianity that are untouchable.

My favorite among these untouchable aspects of our faith is one simply profound idea: There is nothing more attractive than holiness. When somebody actually lives the teachings of Jesus Christ, it is astoundingly attractive to all men and women of goodwill.

In 1950, an Albanian-born schoolteacher stepped into the classroom of silence, sat down with God in prayer, and said, "Lord, the world seems to be a bit of a mess—how can I help?" Her name was Agnes and she felt God was calling her to work with poor people. Agnes didn't go down to her local soup kitchen. She went into the filth and squalor of the worst neighborhoods in Calcutta, India. Each day she woke up, worked with the forgotten ones, the poorest of the poor, the HIV victims, and cared for them as if they were Jesus himself. Over the next twenty years she captured the imagination of the whole world. Most people know Agnes as Mother Teresa. She was loved, admired, and supported by men, women, and children of all faiths, and by those of no faith. Why? How? It's simple, really. There is nothing more attractive than holiness. When someone actually lives the teachings of Jesus in an unqualified way, they capture the imagination of the people of their age, because Holy Moments are universally attractive.

Holy Moments are the answer to all the world's problems. How many thousands of women and men have left their whole lives behind to serve the poorest of the poor, one Holy Moment at a time, because of Mother Teresa's example? Holiness is possible for you, and Holy Moments are incredibly contagious. They change people's lives, and they change the world. Holy Moments literally change the course of human history.

Does the world need changing? It sure does. What does the world need? It needs millions of Holy Moments. How many will you contribute?

The first Christians changed the world. We have talked about how they did it and the challenges they faced. But there is one thing I would like to draw special attention to before we move on. The early Christians had something the people of their time needed and wanted. When someone became a Christian during those early years, they became a member of a dynamic community that provided both spiritual and temporal benefits and protections.

The early Christians redefined their lives by allowing the teachings of Jesus to rearrange their priorities. This manifested in very real and practical ways. They became kind, generous, affectionate, caring, and patient. But they did it together, as communities. So, both as individuals and as communities, they were living life in a very attractive way. As a group, the first Christians presented a radical alternative to the people of their time, who were stuck in a system that treated everyone but the elite like animals, rather than like precious human beings.

Let's take a look now at how that same dynamic is about to play out in our own place and time.

HISTORY IS PRESENTING CHRISTIANITY WITH A NEW OPPORTUNITY

Jesus was the long-awaited Messiah, who preached wisdom that was both mystical and applicable to daily life while at the same time being accessible even to the uneducated. He performed countless miracles, was publicly crucified, and rose from the dead. Beyond all this, a number of other practical factors contributed to the rapid adoption of Christianity. One was the staggering contrast between what Christianity had to offer and what the culture at large was offering the average person. This contrast created an opportunity.

Christianity gave people hope for this life and the next. The great looming darkness that hung over the people of antiquity was their belief that when you died, that was it. It is also a belief that is gathering momentum in our times. Christianity heralded the good news that there is life after death.

When Christianity first came about, it offered people new life both practically and spiritually. It offered people new life in this world and the next world. In a culture of hopelessness, Christianity offered people hope. The practical nature of Christian love and community was so powerful that it opened people's hearts to Jesus and the possibility of eternity.

A very similar opportunity is being presented to Christianity today. The current secular culture is bankrupt—and becoming more so with every passing day. Today's culture is becoming harsher, colder, increasingly brutal, and plagued with an attitude of every man and woman for themselves. People are starting to see this, and they are fed up.

Christianity has always been about attraction rather than promotion. As modern Christians, we need to dedicate ourselves to creating Holy Moments, to recognizing the extraordinary in the ordinary, and to living beautiful lives of simple holiness defined by gentleness, humility, thoughtfulness, generosity, courage, kindness, service to our community, and hospitality. In this way the world will beat a path to our doors, begging for a chance to belong to our dynamic Christian communities. We will have something they desperately need and want.

But this is not how we are living our lives as Christians today, and it's not how our communities are engaging with society. Christians are not perceived by society as gentle, humble, thoughtful, generous, courageous, kind, and hospitable. This is all beautiful, attractive, and positive. So why do so many people today find Christians and Christianity repellent? Why are so many people disgusted with Christianity today? Why do so many people see it as something negative that the world would be better off without?

This portrait has been very effectively painted by secularism, but we have played right into the culture's negative narrative about Christianity by settling for mediocrity spiritually and not striving to live more authentic Christian lives. As a result, we have an identity crisis. How we got here may serve in helping us resolve it, but our focus needs to remain firmly placed on fixing the problem. The crisis is most simply described like this: most people think Christians and Christianity are very different than we are in reality. We need to show the people of our time what it truly means to be Christian, by living authentic Christian lives.

This crisis is the natural result of us not living the Christian faith dynamically enough to convince society that what they have been told about us is lies. This has been furthered by our desperate need to be loved and accepted, which has led us to choose to live in ways that cause us to blend in with people of no faith or opposing faiths.

The first Christians differentiated themselves from society. Modern Christians blend in.

The great paradox is that we don't stop blending in by making it about us. The way to give birth to a new and more authentic image of Christianity is to make it about them. Over the past twenty-five years I have visited churches in more than fifty countries. So many people, so many places, so much goodness, joy, and generosity; but also so much selfishness, pain, greed, and injustice. But mostly what I experienced was people just trying to make life work. This has led me to a theory that I believe is central to the modern re-birth of Christianity. It seems to me that the people who show up to church on Sunday and those that don't show up to church all have the same ten things on their minds. If we can speak powerfully and practically to people about these ten things, we will change the world . . . again.

Here's my best guess at what the ten things are:

1. *Relationships:* Married or single, relationships are central to people's lives. Life is relationships. Most people want their primary relationship to improve, but they don't know how to make it happen. Many have suffered torturous divorces. Those who don't have someone might be asking: Will I ever find someone? Those who are married may be asking: How can we have a better marriage? Does she still love me? Is he having an affair? Is she about to leave me?

2. *Family:* Parents want to know how to be better. They have so many deeply personal questions about parenting, and few places to turn with them. No family is like the Christmas card picture. Every family has something going on that they wouldn't want to see on the front page of the newspaper tomorrow morning. At any given moment most families have a wayward child—who usually grows out of it, but not before causing great grief and anxiety for the parents. There is always something going on between siblings. Then there is the fifteen-year-old girl walking into church on Sunday morning thinking: How am I going to tell my parents I am pregnant?

3. *Health:* Everyone knows somebody with serious health issues. You'd be amazed how many people are taking care of an elderly parent or a special-needs sibling or child on top of all their other responsibilities. You have the person who wants to scream to an indifferent world: I just found out I have cancer! You have millions of women dealing with menopause who feel desperately alone.

4. *Work:* We spend most of our lives working, and most people are not very happy at work. They might be saying to themselves: My boss is a jerk. My colleagues are bullies. They

are laying people off again and as a white male in my fifties I am a target. Are they going to fire me? My coworkers are always competing with me and it takes all the fun out of work. How do I bring more meaning to my work?

5. *Money:* We use money every single day of our lives. How do I discern if I should or shouldn't buy something? How do I resist the peer and cultural pressure to adopt a lifestyle that won't help me or my family become the-best-version-of-ourselves? What's the best way to save money? How much should I save? How should I invest? Will we have enough for retirement? How will I ever pay off this credit card debt? What will my husband or wife say if he or she finds out? Do I have a moral obligation to save? How do I decide how much money to give away? What cause am I most passionate about supporting financially? Should I take a job I know I will hate because it pays more money?

6. *Addiction:* There is hardly a family on the planet now that has not been impacted in some way by this grim reaper. People sit in church every Sunday thinking about their own addictions, which they feel completely helpless about and are desperately afraid other people will find out about. We are all addicted to something: drugs, alcohol, food, other people's attention, pornography, shopping, vanity . . . the list is endless, but you know yours and I know mine. Other people sit in church feeling helpless about the addiction someone they love is battling or refusing to battle. Addiction will be one of the biggest issues of the next fifty years.

7. *God, spirituality, and church:* Whether people go to church or not, these things are on their minds to varying degrees. What is the meaning of life? What can I do to grow spiritually? What is God calling me to at this time in my life? Why don't I like

myself? Both those who go to church and those who don't all have to deal with the guilt they experience about the actions of their lives they are not proud of or that they regret. The amount of self-loathing, even among Christians who believe in a loving and forgiving God, is staggering. Does God really exist? Did Jesus really say all those things? Is heaven real? Great faith and great doubt go hand in hand.

8. *Fear:* We are all afraid of something. Every person who crosses the threshold of church on Sunday is afraid of something, and they come hopeful that God will liberate them from that fear. We fear the future. We fear the past will come back to haunt us. We are afraid of growing old, afraid of retiring, worried about what we will do with all that time, afraid we will run out of money, afraid of terrorism, afraid we will end up in a retirement home and our children will forget about us, and so much more. Did I waste my life? We are afraid, which is no doubt why the most common phrase in the Bible is "Do not be afraid!"

9. *Hopes and dreams:* No matter how young or old we are, we have dreams for ourselves and for those we love. Freedom of choice is hands down the greatest ability God has given us, but the ability to dream is a close second. We have this astounding ability to look into the future and envision something bigger and better, and then come back to the present and work to bring about the dream we envisioned. Extraordinary! It's time to dust off those forgotten dreams and cast aside those self-imposed limitations.

10. *The question:* Every single person is grappling with a question right now. I know what my question is, and you know your question. We have read about it, and perhaps we've asked people we respect for advice. But what we are yearning for is a

deeply personal answer to our deeply personal question. Each and every one of us is waiting on God for that deeply personal answer to our question.

These seem to be the ten things on people's minds. I'd love to write you a book about each of them; so many books to write and so little life. These ten things are very human things. People are just trying to make their lives work. They have little or no interest in debates about the intricacies of Christianity. They are just trying to get by and be good people.

It is striking to me as I read about the life of Jesus that he always seemed to deal with people's human concerns and needs before he preached to them. He fed them and then preached to them. He healed someone and then spoke to that person and the crowd about the lesson behind his healing. His parables were about topics that the uneducated people of those times were dealing with every day, like sheep, coins, the needy, and disputes between neighbors.

What strikes me about the ten things is that we don't spend anywhere near enough time talking to people about these topics, and we don't minister to their needs in these areas at the level we should. Tragically, I can't even remember the last time any of these topics were addressed in a truly practical way in the Sunday message at my own church.

Every Sunday, every person who crosses the threshold into church comes looking for answers and carrying a burden of some type. There is a beautiful quote that has been attributed to a dozen people, but regardless of who said it or wrote it, there is a profound truth contained within it: "Be kind, because everyone you'll ever meet is fighting a hard battle." What hard battle are the people who live under the same roof as you wrestling with? What hard battle are the people you work with fighting? Each of the people next to you, in front of you, and behind you at church on Sunday has their own heavy burden too.

It is for this reason that one of our basic human needs is encouragement. We all need to be encouraged. I cannot tell you how many times I have wanted to walk away from ministry. I can't tell you how often I have felt I was wasting my time and having no impact. But then a note would arrive about how this book or that book had changed someone's life, encouraging me to press on.

If encouragement is a basic need of each and every human being, it is also the responsibility of each and every one of us to do what we can to encourage each other. Encouragement is also one of the primary responsibilities of the Church and every Christian community. You don't help people get to heaven by discouraging them. Every time someone walks into one of our churches, they should be crossing the threshold of hope, and every time they walk out of our churches, they should be crossing that same threshold filled with hope and encouragement.

Is that happening? No. That's part of the problem. There are essentially two parts of the identity crisis Christianity faces today. First, as individuals we tend to be fairly bad advertisements for Christianity, because we have become comfortable with our mediocrity and are not passionately creating Holy Moments. The second part of the problem is that our churches are not temples of hope and encouragement.

We don't have a reputation for helping people with their real and immediate needs, so they have stopped coming to church, and in many cases they've written Christianity off. We are not meeting people where they are and leading them to where God is calling them to be.

What percentage of your church's activities take place on church property? In most cases the answer is more than 90 percent. In far too many cases the answer is 100 percent. We have built some amazing church facilities and campuses, and that is a good thing. But the mentality that accompanies these amazing facilities can be a country club mentality rather than one of a Christian community that is mission driven and passionate about transforming the world starting right there in your suburb, city, or state. What is your church community doing to reach the un-churched? If the answer is little or nothing, you probably have something that resembles a country club more than a church.

If we are serious about transforming the culture, we need to get out in the culture. We need to stop spending so much energy trying to get people to come to us, or howling at the moon bemoaning the fact that they have stopped coming to church, and get out among the people. That's what Jesus did. It is time to get out of the glorified Christian ghettos we have built and reengage the people of our time with a fascinating conversation about life, death, eternity—but first we need to talk to them about whatever they are struggling with right now.

Differentiating ourselves as Christians is not about us; it's about them. God wants us to serve the people of our own place and time, and he wants us to serve them powerfully. How? The solution is clear: with Holy Moments. We will reestablish our credibility in society by changing people's lives and the world one Holy Moment at a time.

Holy Moments will differentiate Christians faster than you can even imagine, because Christianity is being presented with the same opportunity the early Christians leveraged to facilitate its rapid adoption in the first century. There is no contest between what authentic Christian communities have to offer and what this distorted and morally bankrupt modern secular culture has to offer people.

The key is Holy Moments. Holy Moments bring to life Christian values, character, and virtue. These values and virtues embody how we yearn to be treated as human beings. By treating people with good character, values, and virtue, we remind them of what too many of them have never discovered: We are children of God, and along with that comes a birthright to be treated with love, kindness, and dignity.

This is the most significant fact in the history of Christianity: Whenever and wherever you find men, women, and children striving to create Holy Moments, Christianity has always thrived.

EVERYDAY MIRACLES

A thousand years ago, a missionary was visiting a village on a small island deep in the Amazon, when he came upon three old friends talking, singing, and laughing.

The missionary approached the men and asked them, "Do you pray?"

"Oh, yes, padre!" they replied.

A little surprised, the missionary inquired, "How do you pray?"

"We only know one prayer," the men confessed.

"Which prayer is it?"

The three men looked at each other and then hung their heads humbly. "You would not know it. It is not like the prayers you pray, sir."

"Never mind that," said the missionary. "I am curious about this prayer."

The men didn't say anything, their heads still hanging toward the ground as they sat in a circle around their fire.

"Come, men, tell me, who taught you this prayer?" the missionary inquired.

One of the men mumbled, "We taught it to ourselves."

"Will you share your prayer with me?"

"Very well," said one of the men. "Each morning and each evening, before we work and before we eat, we pray: 'God, you are three; we are three. Have mercy on us.'"

"This is a beautiful prayer," the visitor said to the three men, "but let me teach you a prayer that God prefers." He taught them an ancient Christian prayer.

"This is a prayer that God answers?" the three men asked.

"It is indeed," the missionary confirmed.

The three men graciously thanked the visitor and asked for his blessing. "Come, padre," they said. "You will eat and drink with our families this night, and every night while you are here on the island. We have a room where you can sleep and read and pray, and if there is anything else you need during your visit, just whisper it in one of our ears and we will be sure you have it as soon as possible."

The missionary stayed on the island for three weeks, teaching the people about God and his ways and instructing them how to pray. He noticed that the three men were held in great esteem among the community, and many people came to them seeking advice.

Every time the missionary needed something, one of the three men would appear with it before he even asked. It was as if they knew what he needed before he knew. Their hospitality was so deep and true.

Three weeks later, as his ship sailed out of the harbor, the missionary saw the three men again, only this time, to his amazement, they were walking across the surface of the water toward the ship. "Wait, padre, wait!" one of them called out to him. "Teach us one more time the prayer that God prefers. We have forgotten the words."

The missionary hung his head, not in humility, but in shame. Waving farewell to the three men walking toward him on the water, he said, "Never mind. Your own prayer is just fine."

The three friends turned and walked back to shore. And as the ship sailed toward the horizon, the missionary begged God's forgiveness for not recognizing the extraordinary in the ordinary, for not recognizing the beautiful, simple holiness hidden in the three men's gentleness, humility, thoughtfulness, generosity, kindness, service to the community, and hospitality.

***

If you could perform any one of Jesus' miracles, which would you choose? Would you walk on water? I know a lot of college students who would turn water into wine. I know a lot of people who would feed the hungry of the world by multiplying loaves and fish, and others who would heal a loved one. Jesus' first disciples saw him performing all these miracles, and yet what amazed and impressed them the most was the way he treated and forgave his enemies. Forgiveness is a Holy Moment.

Jesus predicted his followers would do things even greater than he did himself. I wonder what he had in mind. All I know is that we are living in a wounded world full of wounded people. Every day I meet people in real need of a miracle. But they are other people in other places. Let's begin with you.

"How are you?" People ask us this question all the time. It's an important question, and it is worthy of some reflection and introspection. The problem is so many people ask us the question and we reply, "Fine," or something similar so often that we start to believe our trivial answer to this important question. So, how are you really? When was the last time you really thought about it? Are you thriving or are you just surviving? Are you focused and energized or scattered and tired? Do you like your life? If you don't, do you know what you don't like about it? Do you actually know what you need and want?

Sometimes we are just sleepwalking through life, completely unaware of the extraordinary people, moments, and possibilities that surround us. When that happens, life loses its flavor.

In those times we need a great friend to tap us on the shoulder, nudge us, or shake us and say, "Wake up!" I've been there. I was there last year again. I've had cancer three times, but last year was the worst year of my life. It was the first year in my life that I wasn't able to say, "This year was better than last year." That shook me. I have a bestselling book about chasing your dreams and helping other people accomplish theirs, but I had stopped dreaming. I threw a few pity parties for myself. I got sad, started second-guessing myself about just about everything, felt betrayed and began feeling down, fell into the trap of becoming overly focused on myself, felt discouraged, and just generally was a bit lost. I don't know how he picks his moments, but at just the right time I felt God's hand on my shoulder, encouraging me to wake up, look around, get grateful, focus on the basics, and start living again.

Life is for living, and the best living is done amid the ordinary things of each day. The modern culture's disdain for the ordinary and worship of the extraordinary has rendered us oblivious to the amazing things in front of us, around us, and within us right now.

The three old men in the story lived lives of gentleness, humility, thoughtfulness, generosity, kindness, service, and hospitality, and they were filled with lightheartedness and joy. You can answer for yourself, but I want more of what they had and less of what I have. The three old men lived simple lives. There is a lesson there for me, and perhaps for you too. Every time I make a conscious effort to simplify my life, I become a-better-version-of-myself, I breathe easier and deeper, and life is better. But the world is constantly trying to heap complexity upon me, and I allow it to. I let this happen. I am no victim. My life is my own, to live and to answer for.

Talking to other people, I discovered that I wasn't the only one feeling this way. The more I talked to people, the more I realized that so many were suffering under the unbearable weight of situations that were uniquely their own but that also shared many of the themes of my own struggle.

I don't like alarm clocks. Just the name disturbs me. Who wants to start the day alarmed? But when you check into a hotel, they often ask you if you would like a wake-up call. I like that. We all need a wake-up call from time to time. I needed one last year. Maybe you need one right now. It is just so easy to fall into the mode of sleepwalking through life.

It's time to wake up. It doesn't matter when you fell asleep, or why. It is time to wake up now. It is time to recognize the beautiful miracles that surround us every day. The three old men in the story could walk on water, but I'm a practical man. I'd rather share a great meal with friends than be able to walk on water. I wouldn't trade one hug with any of my children for the ability to walk on water. I'd rather wake up tomorrow and have one more day of life than walk on water today and die tonight. The air we breathe, the water we drink, the smile of a stranger, making love, taking long walks in quiet places, playing catch, reading great books, sitting with God and soaking up all the love and wisdom he wants to pour into you . . . these are life's miracles. Every single one is a miracle, as are so many more.

Are you ready to experience some everyday miracles in your life? I think it's time. This is our time—your time and mine. Let's grasp it passionately.

LIVE AN INTRIGUING LIFE

You may have read the story about the three old friends and the missionary and wondered what I was trying to say. The beautiful thing about stories is that they speak to each person in a different way. Ten people could read a story and get ten different messages. All ten messages were in the story, but each person heard what he or she needed to hear. I closed the story by writing, "The three friends turned and walked back to shore. And as the ship sailed toward the horizon, the missionary begged God's forgiveness for not recognizing the extraordinary in the ordinary, for not recognizing the beautiful simple holiness hidden in the three men's gentleness, humility, thoughtfulness, generosity, kindness, service to the community, and hospitality."

We are both the missionary and the three old friends. In any story we gain most when we are able to see ourselves in every character. We each need to beg God's forgiveness for not recognizing the extraordinary in the ordinary, for not recognizing the beautiful simple holiness in people's gentleness, humility, thoughtfulness, generosity, kindness, service, and hospitality. But that is not enough, and too often our spirituality stops there. We also need to seek forgiveness for not recognizing ourselves in the three men and others like them in our own lives, for not recognizing that holiness is possible, and for not recognizing all the other possibilities for love, unity, and goodness that we overlook each day.

Do you feel you are living your life to the fullest? I raise this question because it is impossible to confuse Jesus' invitation to "live life to the fullest" (John 10:10) with a life that is boring and meaningless. I know. You probably don't feel intriguing. That's OK. You might not even think it is possible for you to live an intriguing life. That's OK too. Most people don't.

The definition of *intriguing* is "arousing curiosity or interest; fascinating." It's a lot to ask, isn't it? No. It would be a lot to ask of you alone. But it is not a lot to ask of you plus God. You plus God equals unimaginable possibilities. God is inviting you to live an intriguing life, and the Gospels provide the blueprint for that intriguing life.

Nothing is more intriguing than the love and goodness of God, and no person has ever walked the earth who was more intriguing than Jesus. Christians and Christianity become intriguing when we allow God's love and goodness to flow through us to other people. These are just words on a page, but when someone actually allows God's love and goodness to flow through them, it is astounding, powerful, and intriguing.

Holy Moments are intriguing. When Christians set aside self-interest and put someone else or some cause ahead of their own desires, it is baffling to a selfish culture. The fact that people are baffled is just one proof that they are intrigued.

When a Christian strives to create as many Holy Moments as possible, her life becomes intriguing to almost every person who crosses her path. This truth and intrigue is multiplied when the disparity between the values, character, and virtue of a Christian is vast compared to the values of society at that time. We live in such a time. The values of our culture are at the other end of the spectrum compared to Christian values. This gap creates an opportunity.

Holy Moments highlight this gap. They show that values and virtue—love, goodness, kindness, and courage in the face of abuse and injustice—are the only path to lasting happiness in this ever-changing world. They prove there is another path, another way that most people have never considered, and even more tragically, another path that the great majority of people have never been shown. Every Holy Moment is intriguing.

Goodness, kindness, and generosity freely given in everyday life are intriguing. And as society becomes more jaded, cynical, and convinced that people only act out of self-interest, more and more people will be fascinated by and attracted to the genius of Christianity as they witness the selflessness of these values and virtues. The first Christians captured the imaginations of the people of their times, and we can too.

But we are human beings, and we are experts at coming up with excuses. Our main excuse is: "I am only one person—what can I do?"

What if Abraham Lincoln had used that excuse? How would our country be different today? Winston Churchill, Albert Einstein, William Wilberforce, Nelson Mandela, Mother Teresa, Martin Luther King Jr., William Shakespeare, Leonardo da Vinci, Helen Keller, Mahatma Gandhi, Florence Nightingale, Louis Pasteur, Billy Graham, Francis of Assisi, Jesse Owens, Michelangelo . . . What if any one of these men or women had used that excuse?

You may be thinking to yourself, "Yes, but these were extra-ordinary people with astounding gifts." That's true, and most of us are not called to do things like these men and women did. But even more important to our discussion than these famous people are the millions of anonymous men and women who wake up every day, go out into the world, and strive to live with character and integrity, collaborating with God to create one Holy Moment at a time. They are transforming their families, changing their tiny corner of the world. They will never be famous. Most of these Holy Moments go unnoticed by everyone except God. And yet, every day these people are becoming better fathers, mothers, brothers, sisters, sons, daughters, friends, colleagues, neighbors, and citizens, and in the process they are changing the world for the better with their values, character, and virtue.

But this is just all talk. The heart of the matter is that most Christians don't actually believe we can change the world. It doesn't matter to most Christians today that the first Christians changed the world. Modern Christians don't actually believe they can do it. Consciously or subconsciously, we have convinced ourselves that the culture has simply become too powerful. Even many committed modern Christians don't believe that together we can change the world. So, we wait. We fumble along, pretending to do the best we can and waiting for massive divine intervention in the form of the Second Coming. This is the logic we use to stay lazy and procrastinate about our Christianity.

It makes sense. The idea that the culture has become so powerful that even all the Christians in the world cannot match it is the natural extension of the biggest lie in the history of Christianity. If holiness is not possible, then we certainly can't change the world. It is diabolical genius. It's the perfect way to shut down Christianity, a sure way to neutralize Christians and paralyze whole church communities. It is absolutely brilliant. Only the worst enemy of Christianity could come up with a strategy so silent, subtle, and completely effective. I mean, think about it—this one lie has shut down modern Christianity. One lie has neutralized three billion people. That's genius.

The first problem is we don't believe holiness is possible. The second problem is we don't believe we can change the world. So, what are we doing as Christians? The sad truth is we are just pretending.

The beautiful truth is we can change the world . . . again. In chapter eleven we spoke about how we get a seat at the table again. Now let's move beyond our own personal spiritual transformation and talk about how Christians can change the world today.

The first step is to believe it is possible. The primary reason we don't believe it is possible is because it just seems so insurmountable. When we start thinking about it or even talking about it, we quickly become overwhelmed and abandon the mission. It is also worth noting that most people feel overwhelmed by the culture in their own lives. The mind-set of being overwhelmed is one of the most dominant feelings of our times. It is a very negative and destructive feeling because it tends to shut us down and put us in a state of inaction. Anyone and everything that is evil or prefers evil on this planet wants Christians to feel overwhelmed, because when we are stuck in that negative mind space we tend to do nothing. When this happens, inaction takes hold of us, we throw pity parties for ourselves, and we abandon our mission.

Mission? Yeah, mission. It turns out that as Christians, despite our many disagreements and disputes, we have one collective mission, which is most clearly articulated toward the end of Matthew's Gospel and is often referred to as the Great Commission. Jesus instructed the disciples to go out and transform the world by making disciples of every nation.

About three billion Christians think we can't change the world.

I think we can. Let me prove it to you. What I am about to share with you is not my theory. I'm not the source of this idea; it has its roots in Jesus' strategy to choose twelve disciples and focus his efforts on preparing them. A good friend and a good man shared this concept with me, and now I will share it with you. It is called the principle of Spiritual Multiplication.

What is Spiritual Multiplication? It is a method that Jesus himself chose as the foundation of his ministry, and the strategy he put in place to change the world after he died on the cross, rose from the dead, and ascended into heaven.

It is based on one very simple idea: Invest in a small group of people, teaching them how to create Holy Moments and become disciples of Jesus, then empower each of them to go out and do the same for another small group of people. You collaborate with God to create Holy Moments, and then collaborate with him again to teach other people to create Holy Moments. This was also the model that Paul used to win, build, and send a small group of people like Timothy, all of whom formed the ever-expanding circle of Christian influence and transformation in the early centuries of Christianity.

One of the central criteria necessary to successfully introduce Christianity to someone is not to overwhelm them. In the same way, if we want to successfully send Christians out into the world as disciples, it is important not to overwhelm them.

Now, if I told you I needed you to transform your city, you'd probably be overwhelmed, unless you already knew the principle of Spiritual Multiplication or were delusional. If I told you I needed you to transform your neighborhood, you'd still probably feel overwhelmed—I know I would. But if I told you I just needed you to collaborate with God to develop three disciples, your reaction would probably be, "OK, I can do that!"

But not long after coming to the conclusion that with God's help you could develop three disciples, you'd probably also think to yourself, "But wait a minute—only three at a time? At that rate it will take forever to change the world." I can see how you might think that, but let's take a look at it.

Your mission is to disciple three people. Teach them how to create Holy Moments, and teach them each to disciple three more people. You, plus your three, plus their nine, equals thirteen.

13 x 3 = 39
39 x 3 = 117
117 x 3 = 351
351 x 3 = 1,053

Six cycles to get to one thousand, and from there the numbers begin to add up very quickly. The compounding power of Spiritual Multiplication is astounding.

1,053 x 3 = 3,159
3,159 x 3 = 9,477
9,477 x 3 = 28,431
28,431 x 3 = 85,293
85,293 x 3 = 255,879
255,879 x 3 = 767,637
767,637 x 3 = 2,302,911

It takes just thirteen cycles to hit two million people.

2,302,911 x 3 = 6,908,733
6,908,733 x 3 = 20,726,199

It takes just fifteen cycles to reach twenty million.

20,726,199 x 3 = 62,178,597

62,178,597 x 3 = 186,535,791

186,535,791 x 3 = 559,607,373

559,607,373 x 3 = 1.7 billion

It takes just nineteen cycles to reach one billion people.

1.7 billion x 3 = 5 billion

There are seven billion people alive today. It would take just twenty cycles to reach everyone on the planet. The principle of Spiritual Multiplication is real, it's achievable, and it's not elitist. It is accessible and can be adopted and implemented by the rich and poor, the educated and uneducated, and by men and women of all ages and positions in society. Perhaps most important, it is based on the life, ministry, and teachings of Jesus himself. Spiritual Multiplication is a divine strategy. This is how the first Christians changed the world. People have often wondered how such a small group of people had such an enormous impact. Spiritual Multiplication is the answer. They only *started* as a small group of people.

It's time for us all to stop making excuses and to encourage each other to discover what is possible. It's your turn, and it's my turn. It's time to do our part—to renew our commitment to walking with God, to create Holy Moments, and to start praying for God to lead us to the three people he wants us to disciple.

"I am only one person—what can I do?" Let's banish that excuse from our hearts and minds. You can do your part. Can you change the world single-handedly? No. But don't let what you can't do interfere with what you can do. Do your part. I am sure there were lots of Germans around the time of Hitler who used the same excuse. And we all know how that turned out. Many Germans did oppose Hitler and the Nazis, and in most cases they paid with their lives. But I wonder if, had another thousand or ten thousand joined them, they would have changed the course of human history. I don't know what the number is, but I do know that if enough people had stood up in opposition, the Holocaust could have been completely or at least largely prevented. And not just Germans—the rest of the world knew long before they acted. Too many men and women turned a blind eye. "I am only one person—what can I do?" was no doubt a common excuse.

Excuses don't lead to Holy Moments, and every Holy Moment changes the course of history in some way.

Let's turn our attention toward creating Holy Moments, one at a time. It's true, you are just one person—but you are capable of collaborating with God to create thousands of helpful, hopeful, loving Holy Moments that inspire and challenge people to give Christianity one more look. That's all we need. We just need to intrigue the people of today enough to get them to give Christianity another chance.

Let's change the focus of your happiness project to creating Holy Moments and teaching other people to do the same. This is how you will become happier than you have ever been. This is how you will live an intriguing life. Commit to creating Holy Moments. Transform every moment of your day into a Holy Moment. It's the ordinary things that God loves to elevate into extraordinary experiences.

Everyone is looking for elevated experiences. God wants our lives to be filled with them. When we eat, he wants us to taste every single flavor in the food. When we drink a tall glass of clean, fresh, cold water, he wants us to be aware that it is an unimaginable miracle for one-third of the world's population. When your five-year-old daughter or granddaughter comes running up to you, crash-tackles you, gives you a bear hug, and kisses you, God wants you completely present in that moment. When you take a long walk in a quiet place, swim in the ocean, make love, or bite into a crisp apple, God wants you to have an elevated experience. He gives us these elevated experiences by drawing us fully into them and filling us with a supernatural awareness of how amazing these ordinary aspects of life really are. Our quest to create Holy Moments draws us into communion with God in the present moment, creating an explosion of awareness and joy.

It's time for you and me to start living intriguing lives. Our lives can be intriguing in really ordinary ways. It doesn't need to be man-on-the-moon stuff. If you want to intrigue people, offer them authentic friendship. Take a real interest in a small group of people's lives. Offer them care and concern. Deeply listen to them. Most people don't have anyone in their lives who really listens to them. Be that person for them. Authentic friendship has always been the key to sharing the genius and joy of Christianity with others.

Holy Moments are attractive. Holy Moments are intriguing. Holy Moments are contagious.

OUR DIRTY LITTLE SECRET

Our dirty little secret is that we don't actually want our lives to be transformed. Jesus wants to turn our lives upside down, which as it turns out will be right-side up. But we are comfortable with who we are and where we are, and we don't want God all up in our business moving things around, turning things upside down, looking into every dark and dirty corner of our hearts and souls. Don't get me wrong—we want to be Christians, and we want to be considered good or committed Christians (whatever that means). But we are not interested and are certainly not deeply committed to collaborating with God to completely transform ourselves and our lives into the-very-best-version-of-ourselves.

It won't surprise you that this dirty little secret turns out not to be so little after all, and of course it is yet another extension of the biggest lie in the history of Christianity. That lie and all the extensions that are the natural consequence of the lie lead us to one place: the big fat mediocre middle. We have become comfortable with our mediocrity. Our lives have become mediocre.

Our Christian communities have become mediocre. That's why people are not intrigued.

The world wants you to become fat, dumb, and lazy. The world isn't interested in helping you become the-best-version-of-yourself. While Jesus may not have mentioned the big fat mediocre middle, he did speak clearly about salt that loses its taste and our call to be the light of the world, and the book of Revelation speaks about being vomited from God's mouth for being neither hot nor cold, but lukewarm—like the mediocre middle. Sadly, once we accept the lie that holiness is not possible, there is nowhere else to go. Acceptance of the lie always leads to the mediocre middle. This is just one of the reasons why Jesus encourages us to take the narrow path and to enter through the narrow gate. "Small is the road and narrow is the gate that leads to life" (Matthew 7:14).

Our dirty little secret is: we don't want our lives transformed. So all our efforts to better the world are thwarted because we have given up our red-hot center of influence. You have the most influence over yourself. If you abandon your center of influence, the impact of everything else you do will be limited.

We also don't really want our local church communities transformed. We have become comfortable here too. We would like to change a few things around here and there, but these changes are born from our own selfish preferences, not from a passionate desire to change the world.

And don't get me wrong; we do want to make some changes personally too. I call it tweaking. We are not interested in transformation, but we want some tweaking. That's right, we want God to tweak a few things in our lives and in our community, so we pray for tweaking.

Avoiding transformation has a very real impact on our spirituality. Once we abandon the transformation that is the Christian life, our focus falls on tweaking; our spirituality becomes mediocre and very self-centered. Then we start praying for tweaking: Dear God, please tweak this . . . and please tweak that . . . and tweak my spouse . . . and tweak my spouse again because it didn't take the first time . . . and tweak my kids . . . and tweak my boss . . . and tweak my colleagues at work . . . and tweak my son's soccer coach . . . and tweak my daughter's schoolteacher . . . and tweak our pastor . . . and tweak the politicians . . .

We pray for tweaking. I suspect 90 percent of prayers in this country today are tweaking prayers. This desire for tweaking is selective and selfish, while transformation is total and selfless. We pray for tweaking, and then we have the audacity to wonder why or even complain that God doesn't answer our prayers. Why doesn't he answer our prayers? The reason is very simple and clear: God is not in the business of tweaking. God is in the business of transformation. And he is open for business twenty-four hours a day. Anytime you are ready, he'll be ready and available. He has been waiting, in fact. It's time to start praying prayers that God wants to answer, but first, let's explore a question.

If Christians believe the Bible is the inspired Word of God, why don't they spend more time reading and studying it? From time to time both Christians and non-Christians will debate this question, and for the most part, they come to the same conclusions: People don't know where to start; they are intimidated by the various types of literature; they are afraid of misinterpreting the message; and of course, the ever-famous catchall, people are too busy.

Another reason we don't read the Bible is the same reason so few people have really dynamic relationships in society today: we have become an increasingly impatient society. The Bible isn't like other books. It requires patience. Reading the Bible is like meeting a fascinating person: it takes time to get to know him or her. The more impatient we have become as a society, the more our relationships have suffered. Patience is at the core of any great relationship, because it takes patience to listen and really understand the heart of another person. The Bible helps us know the heart of God and the heart of man. That takes time and patience. It's not a self-help book, in which every line is filled with clichés and step-by-step directives. It is about learning God's heart and learning our own heart.

But I don't think any of these are the predominant reason we don't spend more time reading the Bible. Sure, these all play a role. But in a deeply subconscious way, the main explanation for why we don't read the Bible more is diabolically profound: *We know and believe* that the Word of God has the power to transform our lives. That's right. You didn't misread. It's not that we don't believe; it's that we *do* believe. We know the Word of God has the power to transform our lives, and the uncomfortable, unspoken, and often-avoided truth is that we don't want our lives transformed. Be honest. Do you want God to completely overhaul your life and totally transform you?

Transformation may seem attractive in a moment of blissfully holy idealistic exuberance or in a moment of crisis, but the everyday reality is we like to distance ourselves from the inner work required to bring about such a transformation.

***

Have you ever wondered what God looks for on a résumé? What I mean is, when God is looking for someone to send out on a great mission, what qualities do you think he looks for in that person? I am sure we could each come up with a list of qualities and have a long discussion about which are most important. But then if you compared your list to the types of people God has used to do amazing things throughout history, it probably wouldn't hold up. God baffles us with his choices. The list of people he has chosen for great mission doesn't hold up to any type of human logic. He almost never chooses the people you and I would choose. The more you delve into it, the more fascinating it becomes. He almost never chooses people in positions of authority, wealth, or power, and he almost never chooses the best educated or the most qualified. What criteria does he use? Just one: God uses those who make themselves available to him.

All he asks is that you make yourself available. Like the miracle of the loaves and the fishes, we bring the little we have and God does the rest. Availability is what God looks for in the résumé of our hearts. How available are you to God at this time in your life? Think on it. Pause. It is impossible to measure, but you have a sense. Are you 20 percent, 50 percent, 80 percent, 96.4 percent?

What is holding you back from making yourself 100 percent available to God? What would it take for you to make yourself 100 percent available? What are you afraid of losing or missing out on? What are you unwilling to give up for God? What's the danger of making yourself 100 percent available to him? What is the downside of giving it a try and seeing what happens?

We are all a little insane, I guess. Who holds out on God? What are you holding out for? Is it actually worth it? It takes a particular kind of boldness, selfishness, or mental illness to hold out on God. Resisting him is to resist our truest self. Resisting God is to resist happiness. Do you see the insanity of it all?

Together we can change the world, live intriguing lives, and grasp this historic cultural intersection for Christianity, if we will just make ourselves 100 percent available to God. Can we conjure the willingness to surrender ourselves completely to God? If you have never given it a try, I highly recommend it.

God has a mighty, awesome, wonderful transformation in mind for you. So, if the Spirit is stirring within you, encouraging you to embrace this opportunity with the profound wisdom that this is one of those before-and-after moments in life that you will look back on years from now, then I encourage you to pray a prayer of transformation. One of the most astounding facts about modern Christianity—tragic, actually—is that the great majority of us have never prayed a prayer of transformation.

If you want to see miracles, pray a prayer of transformation. If you would like to see miracles in your own life, pray a prayer of transformation. Here is one I have been sharing with people and using for years:

Lord,
Here I am.
I trust that you have an incredible plan for me.
Transform me. Transform my life.
Everything is on the table.
Take what you want to take and give what you want to give.
I make myself 100 percent available to you today.
Transform me into the person you created me to be,

so I can live the life you envisioned for me at the beginning of time.

I hold nothing back.

I am 100 percent available.

Lead me, challenge me, encourage me, and open my eyes to all your possibilities.

Show me what it is you want me to do, and I will do it.

Amen.

If you want to see miracles, pray that prayer. If you want to see and experience miracles in your own life, pray a wholehearted prayer of transformation. That's a prayer God will answer. In fact, he always answers that prayer. Never once in the history of the world has God not answered a sincere prayer of transformation. We need to start praying prayers that God can easily answer, prayers that he wants to answer. When we want what God wants, it becomes easy for him to answer our prayers. But too often we use prayer in a vain and futile attempt to impose our will upon God.

So what's it going to be—more tweaking, or are you ready for transformation? What will be the hardest thing about letting God transform you and your life?

The butterfly emerges from the cocoon; it is a beautiful transformation. Sometimes destruction comes before transformation. Jesus is all about new life. He loves transformation. Ask him to keep the desire for transformation alive in your heart.

If secretly we don't want God to transform us and our lives, we are probably not going to be that passionate about inviting him to deeply transform our church and community. What is true for the individual is true for the whole.

The biggest lie in history is the one we tell ourselves: Holiness is not possible for me. The communal extension of that lie is: The culture has become so powerful that Christianity can no longer change the world. The reason we are not that passionate about really changing the world in our own place and our own time is because we have accepted these lies and we hide behind our dirty little secrets. We pretend. We hide, hoping nobody will discover our secrets and lies.

So, before you go to bed tonight, I want to challenge you to do two things. First, reflect for a few minutes on these questions: How available have I been to God over the past three or four years? Have I ever made myself 100 percent available to God? What would happen if I did? Then I want you to kneel down beside your bed and pray a prayer of transformation. We should never become so proud that we cannot kneel down beside our bed at night and connect with God.

But let me warn you. If you earnestly pray that prayer, you'd better get ready, because something wonderful is going to happen!

NOW IS YOUR TIME!

Toward the end of each year I like to reflect on the past year and the year ahead. Quite a few of my friends have been doing the same, and we pass around questions to ponder. I thought some of these questions might serve to get us into a place of possibility thinking as we begin the next stage of our journey together. Here are some of the questions my friends and I passed around toward the end of last year.

- What was amazing about this year?
- Whom are you most grateful for this year?
- What accomplishment are you most proud of from the past year?
- What was the most empowering decision you made?
- In what area of your life do you feel the least empowered?
- What emotions would you name to describe this past year?
- What can you do next year to become more childlike?
- What brings you joy?

- Whom did you help this year?
- What dream have you given up on?
- What would you like to have more of this year?
- Do you like the direction your life is heading in?
- What needs to be on your NOT TO DO list this year?
- Are you willing to look at your dark side more than ever before this year?
- Have you given up on some part of yourself?
- If you died tomorrow, how would you like the people who know and love you to remember you?
- If you could accomplish any one thing over the next twelve months, what would you like it to be?
- What would make you happier than you've been at any other time in your life this year?
- How serious are you about making these things happen?

Life is full of possibilities. They are stirring within you. When you are most awake and alert, your own personal possibilities stir deep inside you. How much longer are you going to keep ignoring those possibilities?

***

Truth is beautiful. The truth of nature is beautiful. The truth of your existence is beautiful, even though at times you feel tremendously flawed and broken. Truth is something to be sought, celebrated, embraced, and enthroned in our lives.

Lies are ugly. We all have our own, but they are not who we are, and with God's grace we can walk away from those lies today. Lies give birth to more lies, at every stage filling our hearts, minds, and souls with confusion. Truth brings clarity.

God has an incredible dream for you: He wants you to become the-very-best-version-of-yourself. But he is a patient father who understands your beautiful and difficult humanity, so he wants you to embrace and live this dream a little more each day, becoming a-better-version-of-yourself little by little.

Human flourishing is something that delights God. He is interested in the whole person—physical, emotional, intellectual, and spiritual. God is fascinated with every aspect of people and he loves to see his children flourishing. Are you flourishing? Are you thriving, or are you just surviving? The beautiful truth is it doesn't matter what your answer is to any of these questions, because you can start to turn it all around one moment at a time, beginning now.

The wisdom of this world says that past performance is the best indicator of future performance. It's usually true. The exception is when God gets involved. So let God get involved in your life. Continue to invite him into your life like you did with the prayer of transformation.

People want to flourish and thrive. I know I do. I fail miserably at it so often, but I know it is a deep, deep yearning that won't go away. I'll die before that yearning dies. The older I get, the more I see patterns emerging in my life, in history, in relationships, and in the lives of other people. I'll do something stupid and then think to myself, "I have been doing the same stupid thing for twenty years." Patterns are powerful teachers.

Many years ago I wrote: "People don't do anything until they are inspired, but once they are inspired there is almost nothing they won't do." I believed it then and I believe it now. I have seen it time and time again. Inspiration sets free our pent-up possibilities, filling us with the boldness to live life to the fullest.

There are many ways to be inspired. Music is inspiring. Nature is inspiring. A great speech is inspiring. The birth of a child is inspiring. A well-lived life is inspiring. Parents working hard to support their family inspires me. Smile lines in an old woman's face are beautiful and inspiring. Traveling to different places and meeting different people is inspiring. Movies inspire me. Books inspire me. There are so many ways to be inspired, and for me, well, I guess I've noticed over the years that I need a little inspiration every day.

We are speaking of patterns, and one of the powerful patterns I have noticed in my life is inspiration. All these forms of inspiration I have mentioned are powerful, but the most powerful source of inspiration throughout my adult life has been the voice of God. The most common preface to any sentence in the Bible is "God said . . ." (or some variation of it). God spoke to Adam, Noah, Moses, Abraham, Joshua, Jeremiah, Samuel, David, Nathan, Deborah, Hagar, Miriam, Jonah, Ezekiel, Isaiah, Hosea, Mary, and Paul. And though it is so very easy to overlook, God spoke to every person Jesus spoke to while he walked the earth. We read about many of these encounters in the Gospels. God speaking to us is a deep, beautiful, well-established truth of our faith.

Does God still speak to us today? Indeed. God delights in relationship with his children. It isn't that God has stopped speaking, but rather that we have stopped listening. If we can drag ourselves away from the crazy, noisy, busy world and step into the classroom of silence, God will speak to us in this place and this time. If we step into the classroom of silence for a few minutes each day and make ourselves available to God, he will guide, encourage, and lead us. And the more we make ourselves available to him, the more clearly we will hear his voice.

Learning to recognize patterns in our own life is critical. What I have realized over the years is that when I am listening to the voice of God in my life and trying to walk in his way, I find myself focused, inspired, and energized. But there have been many times when I have ignored the voice of God in my life. I have come to many crossroads where I knew clearly which path I should take but I chose the other path. Sometimes it was for pleasure and often it was because it just seemed like an easier path to take. Those choices never brought me any type of lasting happiness, and almost all of them complicated my life and confused my heart.

This pattern has become so powerfully a part of my life that I have come to the conclusion that it provides a pretty good litmus test. What I mean is that when I don't seem to be focused, inspired, and energized for any prolonged period of time, it's usually a solid indication that I have stopped listening to the voice of God in my life.

It is in the classroom of silence that God illuminates our hearts and minds so that we can see clearly and answer passionately those four questions: Who am I? What am I here for? What matters most? What matters least? With these answers and clarity, God then sends us out into the world to live with passion and purpose.

So, it is time to stop making excuses. We have so many excuses, but at the end of our lives I think all of our excuses are gathered up and placed into two buckets: the too young bucket and the too old bucket. Most people really only have two excuses. They spend the first half of their lives telling themselves, "I am too young for those things," and the second half of their lives telling themselves, "I am too old for those things." And life passes us by in the blink of an eye. Don't let these be your excuses. Whatever your age, I am absolutely convinced that now is your time. Now is *our* time.

Mozart was eight years old when he wrote his first symphony.

Charles Dickens was twelve when he quit school to work in a factory, pasting labels on bottles of shoe polish, because his father had been imprisoned for debt.

Anne Frank was thirteen when she began her diary.

Ralph Waldo Emerson was fourteen years old when he enrolled at Harvard.

Paul McCartney was fifteen when John Lennon invited him to join a band.

Joan of Arc was eighteen when she led the French army to victory.

Bill Gates was nineteen years old when he cofounded Microsoft.

Plato was twenty when he became a student of Socrates.

Dietrich Bonhoeffer was thirty-three years old when World War II broke out. He was lecturing in the United States, but he chose to return to Germany to lead fellow Christians against Hitler and the Nazis. Six years later he was executed at Flossenbürg concentration camp, just two weeks before American soldiers liberated the camp.

Joe DiMaggio was twenty-six when he hit safely in fifty-six consecutive games.

Coco Chanel was twenty-seven when she opened her first store featuring comfortable clothes for women.

Henry David Thoreau was twenty-seven when he moved to the shore of Walden Pond, built a house, planted a garden, and began a two-year experiment in simplicity.

Ralph Lauren was twenty-nine when he created Polo.

William Shakespeare was thirty-one years old when he wrote *Romeo and Juliet*.

Thomas Jefferson was thirty-three when he helped write the Declaration of Independence.

Roger Federer was thirty-six when he won the Australian Open—his twentieth Grand Slam title.

Mother Teresa was forty years old when she founded the Missionaries of Charity.

C. S. Lewis was forty-five when he wrote *Mere Christianity*.

Jack Nicklaus was forty-six when he shot 65 in the final round and 30 on the back nine to win the Masters.

Henry Ford was fifty when he started his first manufacturing assembly line.

Ray Kroc was a fifty-two-year-old milkshake machine salesman when he bought out Mac and Dick McDonald and officially started McDonald's.

Pablo Picasso was fifty-five when he painted *Guernica* and began a new era in the arts.

Dom Pérignon was sixty when he first produced champagne.

Oscar Hammerstein II was sixty-four when he wrote the lyrics for *The Sound of Music*.

Winston Churchill was sixty-five when he became Britain's prime minister and went to war with Hitler.

Nelson Mandela was seventy-one years old when he was released from twenty years in a South African prison. Four years later he was elected president of South Africa.

Michelangelo was seventy-two when he designed the dome of St. Peter's Basilica in Rome.

Peter Roget, after being forced to retire, was seventy-three when he published the first thesaurus, which would become one of the most enduring reference books of all time.

Grandma Moses created her first painting at age seventy-six.

Auguste Rodin was seventy-six years old when he married Rose Beuret, whom he'd met when he was twenty-three and loved his whole life.

John Glenn was seventy-seven when he traveled into space.

Benjamin Franklin was seventy-nine years old when he invented bifocal eyeglasses.

Frank Lloyd Wright was ninety-one when he completed his work on the Guggenheim Museum.

Dimitrion Yordanidis was ninety-eight when he ran a marathon in Athens, Greece.

Ichijirou Araya was one hundred years old when he climbed Mount Fuji.

***

Why do I talk to you about these people? Most of them are not pursuing Christian excellence; some of them are not Christian at all. So why do I mention them as our journey comes to an end? To remind us all that human beings—you and I—are capable of incredible things. But too often we don't even scratch the surface of our capabilities. Too often we get caught in the hustle and bustle of life, fall into a daze, and sleepwalk the rest of our way through life. Or we think we are not among the special people and we are not capable of great things.

But we are wrong. We are capable of great things. Every Holy Moment is a great thing, and you are more than capable of collaborating with God to create Holy Moments. And it turns out Holy Moments are just what people, our society, and the whole world need at this moment in history.

Whether you are sixteen or 116 years old, it doesn't matter. Make yourself 100 percent available to God and he will find a way to work powerfully through you. Your age is his problem. Now is your time.

So get out there and start creating some Holy Moments—one at a time, as many as you can each day—and together, let's bring a new hope to the people of our time. What would society look like if more and more people were focused on creating Holy Moments? The people of our time are hungry for hope; we cannot survive without this beautiful gift. Every Holy Moment gives someone, somewhere the gift of hope.

This world should be different because you were here. We have a human obligation to leave the world better than we found it. This is the essence of stewardship. You don't need to be Martin Luther King Jr., Mother Teresa, or Leonardo da Vinci to leave your mark on the world. Like the three old men, you can leave your mark moment by moment, as you fulfill the ordinary duties of your daily life with gentleness, humility, thoughtfulness, generosity, kindness, service, hospitality, lightheartedness, and joy.

Something wonderful is about to happen. Every Holy Moment triggers a chain reaction of other Holy Moments. And every Holy Moment unleashes hope and inspiration.

Lies breed hopelessness, so we shouldn't be surprised that in our culture of lies so many people feel hopeless. The lie that holiness is not possible creates hopelessness among the one group of people who should never lose hope: Christians.

But truth breeds hope. And the truth is, holiness is possible for you, for me, and for your neighbor, one Holy Moment at a time. We can collaborate with God and create a Holy Moment today. That is amazing grace in action.

Don't let the sun go down today without giving the world a Holy Moment. Holiness is possible. This is the one truth that will bring hope to an age of hopelessness. This is the one truth that will unite Christians to collaborate with God and each other to transform the world . . . again. This is the one truth that will make all Christians people of possibility. If you allow this truth to permeate your thoughts, words, and actions, you will become happier than you have been at any other time in your life. I'll say it again: Something wonderful is about to happen!

ABOUT THE AUTHOR

Matthew Kelly has dedicated his life to helping people and organizations become the-best-version-of-themselves. Born in Sydney, Australia, he began speaking and writing in his late teens while he was attending business school. Since that time, millions of people have attended his presentations in more than fifty countries.

Today Kelly is an internationally acclaimed speaker, author, and business consultant. His books have been published in more than twenty-five languages, have appeared on the *New York Times*, *Wall Street Journal*, and *USA Today* bestseller lists, and have sold more than thirty million copies.

He is the founder and owner of Floyd Consulting, a corporate consulting firm that specializes in increasing employee engagement. Floyd serves businesses of all sizes with its coaching, training, consulting, and keynote speaking services.

His personal interests include golf, live music, literature, spirituality, investing, travel, and spending time with his family and friends.

NOTES